CREATE YOUR OWN ECONOMY

ALSO BY TYLER COWEN

Discover Your Inner Economist

CREATE YOUR OWN ECONOMY

THE PATH TO PROSPERITY IN A DISORDERED WORLD

Tyler Cowen

DUTTON

DUTTON
Published by Penguin Group (USA) Inc.
375 Hudson Street, New York, New York 10014, U.S.A.
Penguin Group (Canada), 90 Eglinton Avenue East, Suite 700, Toronto, Ontario M4P 2Y3,
Canada (a division of Pearson Penguin Canada Inc.); Penguin Books Ltd, 80 Strand, London
WC2R 0RL, England; Penguin Ireland, 25 St Stephen's Green, Dublin 2, Ireland (a division of
Penguin Books Ltd); Penguin Group (Australia), 250 Camberwell Road, Camberwell, Victoria
3124, Australia (a division of Pearson Australia Group Pty Ltd); Penguin Books India Pvt Ltd,
11 Community Centre, Panchsheel Park, New Delhi—110 017, India; Penguin Group (NZ), 67
Apollo Drive, Rosedale, North Shore 0632, New Zealand (a division of Pearson New Zealand
Ltd); Penguin Books (South Africa) (Pty) Ltd, 24 Sturdee Avenue, Rosebank, Johannesburg
2196, South Africa

Penguin Books Ltd, Registered Offices: 80 Strand, London WC2R 0RL, England

Published by Dutton, a member of Penguin Group (USA) Inc.

First printing, July 2009
10   9   8   7   6   5   4   3   2   1

Ⓓ REGISTERED TRADEMARK—MARCA REGISTRADA

LIBRARY OF CONGRESS CATALOGING-IN-PUBLICATION DATA

Cowen, Tyler.
Create your own economy: the path to prosperity in a disordered world / Tyler Cowen.
    p.   cm.
Includes bibliographical references and index.
ISBN 978-0-525-95123-0 (hbk.)
1. Economics—Psychological aspects.   2. Creative thinking.   I. Title.
HB74.P8C68 2009
330.01'9—dc22   2009006935

Printed in the United States of America
Set in Fairfield with Agenda
Designed by Daniel Lagin

CONTENTS

PREFACE

The content of this book has a special meaning for the bad economic times that we are experiencing. I view the book and its message as a path to a better life and it is a path that is especially important today.

When the economy is doing poorly, people "cocoon" and turn to less expensive pleasures. During the Great Depression of the 1930s, people cut back on the expensive evening out and looked to board games, radio, and family entertainment at home. People learned how to do more with less and those tendencies shaped American life for decades. The Great Depression wasn't just an economic event; it was also a cultural shift. And there is another cultural shift going on right now. In down times people exercise more, eat out less and cook more, and engage in more projects for self-improvement and self-education. Usage at public libraries is up and people are spending more time on the internet; once you've paid for your connection most of the surfing is free. These trends are more important than most of us realize and in this book I will tell you why. I will tell you why they are not just short-run trends but why they presage something much deeper about our future.

The challenge is this: As the recession has come, rather than sur-rendering, what can we do to empower ourselves and create a better life? What technologies can we use and how? To whom should we look as the new role models and the new heroes? How can we turn inward and improve who we are and how we organize our internal personal worlds?

This book is about the power of the individual to make a differ-ence and also to change an entire world, whether or not the supposed economic forces are on your side. That's what I mean by "create your own economy."

If you'd like to learn more, please turn the page.

CREATE YOUR OWN ECONOMY

What lies behind us and what lies ahead of us are tiny matters compared to what lives within us.

—UNKNOWN SOURCE

1

THE FUTURE OF THINKING DIFFERENTLY

This book will start and end with the idea of the value and the creative power of the individual. This is the ultimate driver of prosperity in the modern world; it is the power that can get you the best things in life. Our tour in the middle will visit society, technology, politics, economics, culture, and the internet, but the first step on this journey will be one of self-discovery.

One day, about five years ago, something strange happened. One of my blog readers at www.marginalrevolution.com—her name is Kathleen Fasanella—wrote me and asked me very politely and very intelligently to consider if I might be described by either Asperger's syndrome or high-functioning autism. She thought I was, just from reading my writing, and she considered herself an Aspie, the current shorthand for Asperger's syndrome. In her email she pointed out that I keep quite a bit of information in my head in a highly ordered fashion and that I have a command of many small facts in my areas of interest, namely culture and the social sciences. Apparently that was enough to set off her radar.

Now, I receive all sorts of email, so this didn't sink in immediately. At first I found it vaguely insulting, a bit like the "crank" emails

I receive with conspiracy theories about the Federal Reserve System. But I investigated the question further and the more I read about the phenomenon, the more I saw that, while I do not fit the typical public conception of an autistic or suffer from "low social intelligence," I have many of the cognitive strengths and weaknesses of autism. In other words, I have an autistic cognitive style. I've since come to believe that this is a common cognitive pattern, including among some very successful people.

At the time I was very surprised by Kathleen's message. I was a forty-one-year-old upper-middle-class white male who all his life felt like he belonged to the dominant group in American society. Suddenly I was faced with the suggestion that I could be part of a minority, and a very beleaguered minority at that. I have since become comfortable with my affiliation with autism, and indeed proud of it, but it's not a thought I was ready for at the time.

One strong feature of autism is the tendency of autistics to impose additional structure on information by the acts of arranging, organizing, classifying, collecting, memorizing, categorizing, and listing. Autistics are information lovers to an extreme degree and they are the people who engage with information most passionately. When it comes to their areas of interest, autistics are the true *infovores,* as I will call them. Autistics are sometimes portrayed as soulless zombies, but in fact they are the ones with the strongest interest in human codes of meaning. "Joy," "passion," and "autism" are probably not three words you are used to finding together but they are often a close fit.

"We all have our particular areas that we know very, very well" is what one autistic person said to me, and he did not have an advanced degree. Often autistics seek out work that satisfies their passion for information, whether it involves designing new software for a library, conducting a scientific experiment, or ordering ideas in the form of a book or a blog. Mark Donohoo, an autistic, spends a lot of his time studying the statistics of the Atlanta Braves and collecting baseball literature. Or to consider one more stereotypical case, Ethan, an autistic boy in kindergarten, was fascinated with railway schedules and read the schedules all day long online, at least until his mother restricted his hobby. The Metro-North was his favorite train to follow.

The notion of "ordering information" may sound a little dry, but it is a joy in our everyday lives, whether you are autistic or not. It should be familiar to anyone who has enjoyed alphabetizing books on a shelf, arranging photos in an album, finishing a crossword puzzle, or just tidying up a room. It's not that anyone sits down and says "I want to do some ordering now," but rather we are interested in specific features of our world. We have become infovores to help make the world real and salient for us. Ordering and manipulating information is useful, fun, alternately intense and calming, and it helps us plumb the philosophic depths. We are entering a world where the collection and ordering of information has reached baroque, extravagant extremes, and that is (mostly) a good thing. It is a path toward many of the best rewards in life and a path toward creating your own economy and taking control of your own education and entertainment.

As I read more, I began to see that the autistic mind-set about engaging with information is a powerful way to understand the whole world around us. Especially now.

Coping with information involves both cognition and overt behavior. Most of us can't keep track of everything in our minds, so we call upon technology to help us, or as economists would say, we use capital goods. Because of the web, mental ordering has become very cheap and effective and thus it has become a very powerful social force.

Consider the rise in popularity of the iPod or the music-playing iPhone. Compact discs have become secondary and at least in the United States most music is now played on computers and computer-like devices. Having passed Wal-Mart in 2008, iTunes is now the biggest American music retailer. A 2008 survey showed that, when it comes to music, most young people don't think anymore about buying compact discs. My nineteen-year-old stepdaughter, Yana, listens to almost all her music on her computer or her iPod. Her first year in college has come to a close, but to my initial horror it has yet to occur to her that she needs a stereo in her dorm room. The reality is that she has far more control over her musical life than I did at the same age, far more choice, and greater ease of access.

The physical design of the iPod is compelling but the looks are only one part of the appeal. The iPod and other MP3 players are mostly about reorganizing the relationship between music and your mind.

Users organize music into playlists to suit their moods, the friends they are with, or the kind of trip they are taking. Brazilian music gets one playlist, punk rock gets another, and "Songs I Fell in Love To" gets another yet. The "random shuffle" feature is prominent on the choice wheel, precisely because we want to be surprised by the music we hear, yet without giving up our role in controlling the final menu. Friends share and exchange iPods. The iPod is about owning music, classifying music, and identifying with music in new ways.

Your iPod, by arranging your music collection in a new way and giving you new power over its organization, actually makes that music sound better. You think of music as something more important, more worth spending time with, more special, and more of an extension of yourself. When "Bohemian Rhapsody" comes through your iPod ear-buds on random shuffle mode, it can sound wondrous. You reconnect with the whole music listening experience again, as if you were dis-covering the song for the first time at fifteen years old, as I once did. It's well known in marketing circles that the hardest thing to sell con-sumers is "a lump of music"; instead a perceptive supplier will sell a new kind of music listening experience. This gadget brings together two things we love: great music and the deeply personal feeling of "be-ing in control." It's no accident that Guy Hart-Davis's published guide to using the iPod and iTunes fills 508 pages, and without much chaff or waste—and that doesn't include information on the 2008 updates.

The economic structure of the industry has been upended since the advent of iTunes and the iPod. Music superstores, such as the now-bankrupt Tower Records, are in retreat. The music companies were used to a model where they ordered the songs for you, on some-thing called an album. That's mostly gone too. Most fans and con-sumers do the ordering on their own rather than pay a musical group or a company to do it for them. In other words, a lot of the value pro-duction has been moved inside the individual human mind.

The iPod offers inferior or at best equal sound quality to most traditional stereo systems (you can download higher-density, better-sounding songs, but this takes up lots of disk space and hardly anyone does it). The fact that most listeners don't seem to care is another way of understanding what the iPod is about, namely reorganizing how the mind controls and orders music. Sound quality is an afterthought.

Compare the iPod to the music subscription services—such as Rhapsody and Napster, among others—that failed to lead the market. The subscription services had a good selection and at very reasonable prices, as they allowed listeners to hear the music they wanted, when they wanted. But you couldn't own and manipulate the songs in the same way as with an iPod. You couldn't control, shape, share, and reorganize the musical experience in the same way. The subscription services failed to generate much love, precisely because they offer less culturally useful software. When Rhapsody announced a total reorganization of its service in June 2008, it pointed in the direction of the iTunes/iPod experience.

Behavioral economists sometimes write of human beings as subject to "framing effects," meaning that the presentation of the alternatives influences our choices. For instance we often choose more conservatively if the very same opportunity is described to us as a gain of something rather than as a loss of something. Or the presence of a very-high-calorie item on a menu—which we don't order—makes us feel less guilty about later getting dessert. Usually the presumption is that framing effects are to be avoided. To be sure, many framing effects are irrational but framing effects help put the guts into our lives. We spend time and energy framing things in the right way so that we can enjoy them more or learn more from them. Framing helps us care and it gives meaning to our experiences. If you can't afford that new Jaguar sedan, and you are instead battening down your economic hatches and cocooning at home, good framing is how to make that work for you. Good mental ordering is how you can create your own set of frames and thereby create your own economy.

Framing and ordering shape even the social side of our lives. I really do feel more connected to the people who are my (well-ordered) Facebook friends or whom I follow on Twitter or in the blogosphere. Ordering people in these ways makes me think about who they are and why they are important to me.

The highly social Facebook makes us all infovores about our friends. Not only must you choose who is a friend and who is not, but you can add lots of structure to the mental universe of your friends. You can send them periodic iconlike gifts or ask them to take tests of similarity with you or try to befriend the "coolest" people. You can present and order every movie you have seen and every book you have read or every photo you have taken. You can have your web "tags," blogs, diaries, and other forms of your personal web data and usage fed right into your Facebook page, thus making some of your ordering virtually effortless. Your "news feed," now on the main Facebook personal page, orders what your friends are up to.

The average participant on the social networking site Facebook—and circa 2008 there are well over sixty million users—has 164 friends and visits the site numerous times a day. My acquaintance Alissa, an intensely social user of the service, has currently 294 Facebook friends and visits the site several times a day. She posts photos (110 at last count), exchanges messages, responds to party invitations, joins or quits "Facebook groups," and of course recruits new friends. She "defriends" those people who do not keep in touch. At last count Alissa was a member of thirty-two Facebook groups, including Save the Polar Bears, Addicted to Starbucks, and Kids Who Hid in Dept. Store Clothing Racks While Their Mom Was Shopping. That's what I call having an ordered online existence. Today it is the norm, not the exception.

Some users try to order as many different "friends" as they can. Steve Hofstetter once acquired about two hundred thousand friends on Facebook, if only to have the largest number of friends in the history of the service. He started off with a goal of ten thousand friends, then hit fifteen thousand friends, and eventually expanded to a hundred thousand and then two hundred thousand friends. At the time he had more than 1 percent of the college student population of Facebook as his friend. Eventually Facebook reset his profile because it got to the point that his page slowed down the loading of Facebook for other users. Facebook has since decided to limit the number of friends you can have to five thousand (circa 2008). But if you really like Steve, even if you can't be his friend you can join his Facebook group; there is no limit on the number of members. Steve, by the way, has since decided to become a professional comedian.

So who is Steve Hofstetter? The most sociable guy in the world? Or an information junkie who accumulated nominal friends on Facebook for fun? Maybe he is a bit of both. Hofstetter himself noted: "Facebook's programmers were not expecting to run into someone quite as obsessive as Steve Hofstetter." There is even a Facebook group called "I'm not addicted to Facebook." It is not uncommon for people, especially young people, to check Facebook fifteen times a day or more.

Totspot is billed as a Facebook for children. Parents set up profiles for their babies, who are sometimes no more than a few months old, and connect those profiles to the profiles of other babies, typically the babies of their friends. You can list your baby's favorite foods, books, and nicknames. Some parents are visiting and updating the profiles once a day or more. And it's not just Totspot; there is also

Lil'Grams, Kidmondo, and others. Odadeo helps you keep track of your pledges to be a better dad and whether you have followed them.

For some people it's not enough to catalog the babies of their friends. Many people also order their different social networking services, using FriendFeed, Fuser, 8hands, Gathera, and Secondbrain. On Wikipedia it's called "social network aggregation."

Fundamentally the relationship between human minds and human cultures is changing. Today culture is not just about buying and selling straightforward commodities such as books or compact discs. Each day more fun, more enjoyment, more social connection, and indeed more contemplation is produced on Facebook, blogs, YouTube, iPods, eBay, Flickr, Wikipedia, and Amazon.com—among other services—than had been imagined twenty or even ten years ago. No matter what the medium, much of the actual value today comes from readers, viewers, students, and consumers, as an "add-on" to what they are sent by corporations. More and more, "production"—that word my fellow economists have been working over for generations—has become interior to the human mind rather than set on a factory floor. Even when a major media corporation produces the pixels, viewers and listeners use their mental ordering to create the meaning and the interpretations, and that is where most of the value lies.

There is quite literally a new plane for organizing human thoughts and feelings and we are jumping on these opportunities at an unprecedented pace. If we look at how culture is supplied, distributed, and enjoyed, the last five years have brought more change than any comparable period in human history. The proper use of entertainment and education has become the most fundamental social enterprise.

In essence we are using tools and capital goods—computers and the web—to replicate or mimic some of the information-absorbing, information-processing, and mental-ordering abilities of autistics. You'll read or hear some speculative claims about how using the web is "changing our brains," or rewiring our brains, through the medium of neuroplasticity, but my message is more straightforward. The web allows us to borrow cognitive strengths from autism and to be better infovores, even if it doesn't rearrange any of the wiring between our ears.

We're applying mental ordering wherever we can. Earth itself can be viewed, classified, tagged, and mentally organized like never before. North Korean military installations and some other bits aside, Google Earth creates a tile-by-tile mosaic of the entire planet. There is tilt, zoom, rotation, and 3-D portrayals of major cities, all organized by zip code, address, or latitude and longitude. The layers function tells you where the public parks are, where an earthquake is most likely to strike, whether political refugees are streaming into a region, and whether you can view an area through a live webcam. Rowdy British teens use Google Earth to find neighbors' empty pools to crash and commandeer for parties. Or you can embed your favorite YouTube video inside a picture of almost anywhere on the planet—you can listen to blues while watching the Mississippi Delta—or you can tour Disney in three dimensions. When you get bored with Google Earth, move on to Google Sky.

Delicious, which is now used by at least three million people, helps you create your own multidimensional website for indexing content on particular topics. You can tag websites and photos and come back to them whenever you want, thereby generating easy access. It's also easy to visit the links and photos that other people have marked with the same keywords. You create your own private encyclopedia of content and meaning, but on the web rather than in your mind.

Personal photographs have become one of the most central manifestations of contemporary culture. It's not that the quality of the photos is always so high, but rather that the pictures are used to weave together a memorable emotional narrative of family, vacation, and personal experience. The web service Flickr helps you order your photographs and share them with others. Right now Flickr offers more than two billion images, all laid out in a searchable order. I searched my own name and in less than two seconds I found four photos tagged (by other users) under my name, including a photo of myself and also a photo of a large stack of books. The new word for such sites is "folksonomy," which combines the two roots of "folk" and "taxonomy."

What is Wikipedia but a vast ordered, intellectual space to collate and effectively present the factual and analytical knowledge of mankind? It is one of the most impressive projects of ordering that human beings have undertaken.

It would be a mistake to think that our new infatuation with information and ordering is about the mind at the expense of the body. Even when we do the most physical, the most exuberant, and the most sensual life activities, we are still imposing new mental orders on our choices.

The website Bedpost (www.bedposted.com) helps users map their sex lives online. The instructions are pretty clear: "Simply log in after every time you have sex and fill out a few simple fields. Before long, you'll have a rolling history of your sex life on which to reflect. Use the tagging feature to provide even deeper insight into your activities, and use the partner feature to record as many partners as you encounter."

The location tracker Brightkite organizes where you have been and My Mile Marker helps you record your driving habits, including when you filled up your vehicle with fuel. The Garmin Forerunner 305 GPS watch looks like a regular digital wristwatch. But if you wear it when you run, a record of your exertions can be downloaded to your computer. It keeps a running tally (how many miles did you really run last month?) and it can export information directly to your Facebook account. There is a website—everytrail.com—where you can share your trips with others and automatically "geotag" your photos. Web tracking also is being used to enforce diets, quit smoking, aid or prevent conception, and cure bad habits.

The basic idea behind the new web innovations is to take a blooming, buzzing mass of overwhelming confusion—modern information, in its richness and glory—and impose some local coherence on it, thereby turning it into usable form. That process reflects how we cope every day. But wait . . . it's a familiar principle. For purposes of comparison, Kamran Nazeer, a British lawyer, policy advocate, and author who describes himself as autistic, suggests the following portrait:

> An autistic person might have a different hierarchy, or might have no hierarchy at all of sense data. That's what often happens with autistic people when they feel overwhelmed by their surroundings. It's because they're not forming a hierarchy of

sense data, it's because they're taking on all the sense data, it's random, and as you can imagine, we're always overwhelmed by sense data. But the reason why we don't feel overwhelmed is because we have a hierarchy for sorting them out. I think that what often happens with autistic people is that they don't hierarchize. Either they don't hierarchize in the same way, or they don't hierarchize at all? . . . A lot of autistic people display what I and many other people have called *desire for local coherence*. So because they're not forming a hierarchy of sense data, which ultimately is the only way in which we can stop ourselves from feeling overwhelmed in the world, what they do instead, instead of forming the hierarchy, they ache for some simple way of bringing order to the chaos around them.

For a typical person, you encounter the web, and you feel overwhelmed, but you figure out how to impose some local coherence in your own way, if only by using Google search or going to your "favorite places" bookmarks. You resort to some mental ordering, usually with the aid of technology. At first you're just struggling to keep up, but the more time you spend on the web, the more you are in control. You move from bookmarks to Facebook to Twitter and then to hyperspecialized sites for ordering the details of your life. You move from bewilderment to a sense of increasing mastery.

Economists have studied our species as *homo economicus,* and a few decades ago, when my social science colleagues investigated our game-playing nature, *homo ludens* was born. Today a new kind of person creates his or her very own economy in his or her head. The age of *homo ordo* is upon us.

We're going to come back to the web and what it means for how society is changing, but first let's look at the people who have been the mental orderers par excellence. Whatever the tragedies of autism may be, we can learn a great deal from autistics and from their cognitive *strengths*. They remain a surprising key to understanding where our world has been and where our world is headed.

2

HIDDEN CREATIVITY

To understand what we might learn from autistics, first we need to clear our minds of most of what one tends to hear about autism. As I looked into the autism literature and talked with and corresponded with autistic people, I was shocked to discover how ignorant I was. Forget you saw the movie *Rain Man*. Autism involves many different features of the human condition and is often connected to human tragedy, but I would like you to view autism from another angle. I would like you to consider the possibility that many autistics—and not just savants—have significant cognitive strengths.

Autism is discussed in at least two different and sometimes conflicting ways:

1. Autism refers to some (connected) cognitive abilities and disabilities.

2. Autism is about personality and overt behavior.

There is a very common subset of number 2, namely:

2b. Autism is about having lots of problems and bad life outcomes.

This last sentence represents the prevailing public conception of autism, that it is fundamentally a series of handicaps and disorders. Unless the problems dominate the discussion, there can be no autism, and anyone who suggests otherwise simply doesn't know what autism means. At that point a long series of definitions is trotted out, usually invoking versions of number 2b, to discredit any contrary point of view. Many established definitions, most of all in formal diagnostic manuals, define autism in terms of various "impairments."

Maybe there are some practical reasons for defining autism, and other neurodevelopmental paths, in terms of life problems. For instance some legal and insurance questions are settled by referencing whether an individual has a formal diagnosis. It is the presence of impairments that leads to a diagnosis, which leads to a court judgment (if only potentially), which in turn activates a payment or a legal claim or perhaps an educational classification.

But whatever the practical uses of such schemes of classification, understanding human neurodiversity in terms of impairments is fundamentally misleading. We are letting our understanding of some very real human beings be determined by formal medical and legal questions. There is a deeper approach that sets autistics into a broader understanding of the human condition, namely as striving people who learn all sorts of wonderful things, know many kinds of joy, and experience tragedies large and small. This understanding is both good for autistics and will help us learn from autistics for our own collective benefit.

Obviously autism often comes with problems. But a correlation should not be turned into a definition, any more than we should *define* sub-Saharan Africa as being full of poor people. If we *define* autism in terms of its problems, we will find it harder to understand how those problems come about, how to remedy them, and how to appreciate and build upon autistic strengths.

There is also an ethical reason why I don't want to define autism in terms of impairments or failed outcomes. I don't want to use the hammer of science to brand a group of people as "inferior" as a preordained social consensus. We've rejected such approaches to race and physical handicaps, precisely because we have, in those other contexts, realized that every individual matters and that negative stereotypes can be destructive. It is time to do the same for autism. No matter what you think is the average or the typical outcome from autism, and no matter how much tragedy from autism you have seen, heard about, or read about, please do not talk or write about autism as if it is like a broken arm, a defect to be repaired or destroyed and nothing but a plague on the world. When you refer to autism you are discussing some very real people, and some of those people are reading your words with great awareness and receiving the message that they are less valuable as human beings simply because of who they are. That's neither good medical practice nor a good philosophic foundation for a society of free and dignified individuals.

With regard to non-autism disabilities, there has been a trend away from portraying disabled people as doomed and pitiful burdens. It is time to apply the same standards to our discussion of autism.

I conceive of autism in terms of a cognitive profile, namely cognitive strengths and weaknesses. The result is that—as you will see—problems will be frequent but many successes and good outcomes appear as well. Most of all, we will better understand the cognitive strengths of autism.

The cognitive understanding emphasizes that autistics differ in the very basic ways they experience the world and how they learn from it. The cognitive profile of autistics is complex but I wish to focus on two cognitive abilities in particular. First, many autistics are very good at perceiving, processing, and ordering information, especially in specialized or preferred areas of interest; I've already discussed this passion for information in chapter 1.

Second, autistics have a bias toward "local processing" or "local perception." For instance an autistic person may be more likely to notice a particular sound or a particular piece of a pattern, or an autistic may have an especially good knowledge of detail or fact, again in preferred areas of interest.

To set off those two features for emphasis, the cognitive strengths of autism include:

- Strong skills in ordering knowledge in preferred areas
- Strong skills in perceiving small bits of information in preferred areas

Overall we've been learning that the cognitive strengths of autism are more significant than people used to think. Just to provide a brief list of such strengths, autistics have on average superior pitch perception, they are better at noticing details in patterns, they have better eyesight on average, they are less likely to be fooled by optical illusions, they are more likely to fit some canons of economic rationality, and they are less likely to have false memories of particular kinds.

Autistics are also more likely to be savants and have extreme abilities to memorize, perform operations with codes and ciphers, perform calculations in their head, learn to read spontaneously, or excel in other specialized cognitive tasks. Autism, however, has cognitive strengths with or without savant-like abilities; non-savant autistics tap into the same sources of cognitive advantage as do the savants, albeit in less extreme form.

A cognitive problem is that many autistics are easily overwhelmed by processing particular stimuli from the outside world. This problem is related to the aforementioned strength of local perception. An autistic might have a very sensitive sense of smell but also be bothered or burdened by what is to his perceptual equipment the overly strong scent of a perfume or a piece of chocolate. Or an autistic might be bothered by an alarm or a siren or by the flickering of fluorescent lighting. Sometimes the feeling of being overwhelmed is so strong that an autistic cannot function well in mainstream society. For instance some autistic people have trouble dealing with mass transit or other noisy, sensory-intensive public settings. For an autistic, the ability to control his or her environment has an especially high value.

Some researchers view autistics as having perceptual equipment turned either "very on" or "very off" rather than modulating at the more typical ranges in between. Some autistics for instance have either unusually high or unusually low sensitivities to physical pain. In this view autistics are a group of people whose "switches" are in unusual or extreme combinations of on or off positions. The thing is, the arrangement of the switches differs across each autistic person and that is one reason why it is hard to make accurate generalizations about autistics as a whole.

A somewhat different understanding of autism postulates that there is less automatic "top-down" control of how sensory perception is processed. So some forms of perception are stronger or more acute, yet again there is the danger of being overwhelmed at the level of perception. In this view the "top-down manager" of the brain plays a stronger role in non-autistics. The autistic interest in ordering information may reflect forces that become stronger when the top-down manager is weaker or turned off.

A number of cognitive problems occur in many autistics at higher-than-average rates. It is common, though by no means universal, that autistics have difficulty with speaking intelligibly or that they are late talkers or that they understand written instructions better than spoken instructions.

Some researchers include "weak executive function" (a bundled function of strategic planning, impulse control, working memory, flexibility in thought and action, and other features) as part of the cognitive profile of autism. Other research focuses on the question of "weak central coherence," or failure to see the "bigger picture." But it seems these are secondary traits, more common in autistic subgroups than in autism per se. The evidence also indicates that high-IQ autistics are quite able to see the big picture when they want to, even if they have a preference for processing small bits of information. When it comes to autism, very often whether a given generalization is true depends on which subgroup of autistics is being considered.

It is a common stereotype that autistics are unaware of the mental existence of other people, but this is a very poor definition of autism. Many autistics do fine on "theory of mind" tests and can understand the intentions of other people quite well. Furthermore many non-autistic children with handicaps, including linguistic handicaps, fail theory of mind tests just as some autistic children do. Theory of mind experiments usually test a complex bundle of human features, including attention-shifting abilities, interpretation of commands, linguistic skills, and common frames of cultural reference. A great number of autistics do find many features of mainstream society and social life quite baffling (I'll return to this question), but it's not because they are zombies with no conception of internal mental life.

In any case, if you take these cognitive abilities and disabilities and stick them into a rapidly evolving market economy, you will get some people who achieve relatively high social status and other people—many others—who end up with much lower status. That's my basic view of autism as a social phenomenon, namely that for reasons rooted in perception and cognition there is a very high variance of outcomes across individuals. That's true whether you look at outcomes in wages, outcomes in IQ, outcomes in scientific achievement, outcomes in music appreciation, and many other measures. The high variance of outcomes means it is easy to find lots of evidence of impairments in autism, but again that's missing the bigger picture.

Understanding autism as more than just impairments does not mean that everything is ideal as it currently stands. It would be a very good thing if many autistic children and adults could develop more of the skills held in greater proportion by the non-autistic. But let us be consistent: I also think it would be good if most non-autistic people could develop some of the skills held in greater proportion by the autistic. As I'll discuss in the next chapter, it is already a fundamental (yet misunderstood) goal of our educational system to teach (non-autistic) people some of the cognitive strengths of autistics.

I am using the words "autism," "autistic," and "autism spectrum" because these days that's how most self-aware autistic people discuss themselves. The word "Asperger's" can be used to refer to a person who has many cognitive traits of autism but fewer developmental difficulties at young ages, little or no delay in language development, and relatively strong verbal abilities. Researchers are split on the question of whether Asperger's is conceptually distinct from autism, but over time the tendency has been to doubt whether a clear line can be drawn and so I will refer to autism unless the context requires reference to when other people use the word Asperger's. Since Asperger's is a more socially acceptable term, many people have encouraged the use of that word and concept, if only for fear of being labeled autistic and becoming outcasts. (You'll find the word "neurodiversity" used in this manner as well.) There's also a more sinister usage of the word "Asperger's." Many people believe that autistics cannot possibly have positive achievements and capabilities. So whenever an autistic does something positive, those people reclassify the autistic as Asperger's in order to save "autism" as a purely negative category. That practice is one reason I don't use the word "Asperger's," although I don't want to pin that fault on the many responsible users of the word and the associated concepts.

You'll also hear the word "nerd" associated with the Asperger's concept. "Nerd" is a sociological term and thus it doesn't map into autism in any simple way. Maybe many nerds belong to a subcategory of autistics but it would be wrong to think that most autistics would be viewed by the world as nerds. Nerds are typically precocious learners and many autistics are perceived as slow or mentally retarded (if only because of difficulties in communicating) even when they are not. The distinction between nerds and slow learners is another good example of the diversity of outcomes within autism.

My views on the cognitive strength of autism are much influenced by my former colleague economics Nobel laureate Vernon Smith. One day Vernon "came out of the closet" and announced to the world on television (later on YouTube, check for it) that he is self-diagnosed Asperger's. He talked of his focus, his persistence, his attention to detail, how he perseverates about his ideas, and how socializing in public can exhaust him. Vernon also attributed much of his career success—he isn't just a Nobel laureate; he is one of the more important and influential laureates—to what he calls his Asperger traits. To date Vernon is probably the highest-status person to make such a public admission. For the most part it fell upon a stony silence and many people don't believe that someone as successful as Vernon could possibly be autistic.

Often outsiders don't see the cognitive strengths along the autism spectrum because they focus excessively on what is highly or easily visible. Autism in the modern world is often about "diagnosis" and "treatment," and that creates a selection bias. Medical professionals control the familiar definitions of autism and they meet those people or parents who come to them for help. It's no surprise that these people and their doctors are focused on life problems. At the same time, many of the autistics with relatively high social status don't want to affiliate with the concept or, more frequently, they are genuinely unaware that they might qualify as autistic in some manner.

Selection biases operate again if you visit the more informal gatherings of self-described autistics, Asperger's, and neurodiverse individuals. The individuals who go to a support group or join an online discussion forum are often responding to some felt needs in their lives or experiencing problems. They would like advice or comfort from similar others. It's good that help or at least consolation is available. But again, focusing on such groups will bias our understanding. The "observable autistics," whether in medical clinics or online, usually aren't the autistics, or the people along the autism spectrum, who hold the highest social status. Again, the universe of studies on autism has evolved to give us a slanted view of what autism is all about.

There are exceptions to this biased picture. Simon Baron-Cohen has done a good deal of work on autistic high achievers; his conclusion is that they are far more common than most people realize, most of all in the fields of mathematics and engineering. He stresses systematizing behavior as an important cognitive strength of autistics.

Craig Newmark, founder of the web forum Craigslist, has written on his blog that his history as a "recovering nerd" is connected to Asperger's. It is perhaps no accident that autistics are known for their attachment to lists as a means of processing, recording, and ordering knowledge. Bram Cohen, creator and former CEO of BitTorrent, also describes himself in terms of Asperger's syndrome. He founded the company at age twenty-nine and BitTorrent has been a pioneer in exchanging digital information over the web; one of his key insights was how BitTorrent could break up files into smaller bits and send through the bits rather than the whole file at once. Cohen mastered three programming languages by the age of sixteen and his work on BitTorrent is regarded as brilliant. The best-known example of an autistic high achiever is Temple Grandin, a woman who has pioneered commonly used improvements in animal treatment and slaughter-houses; her unique cognitive perspective has helped her understand when animals are afraid and how they can be made to feel more secure.

I've yet to see a scientific paper or serious clinical discussion of the autistics who hold political office, work in Hollywood, start web 2.0 companies, or run major U.S. corporations or hedge funds. If you still think such a path of achievement sounds crazy, go to Google and visit the website of the National Association of Blind Lawyers. Handicaps can be overcome or compensated for, especially by talented and determined people who are willing to focus on learning. Thomas Gore of Oklahoma (1870–1949) was a completely blind lawyer and he went on to become a U.S. senator for twenty years.

Or consider this parable: I once met a woman at a lunch party who is, for cognitive reasons, unable to recognize the faces of others. (This condition is known as prosopagnosia and it turns up in many popular books on neuroscience.) This same woman was the one person in the room who remembered who everyone else was. It turns out she has developed a system for remembering people by their clothes and that she applied her system very conscientiously and consistently; without the system she would be lost. People such as myself, who have normal face-recognition abilities, usually have no such system. The result was that this woman—some might call her "handicapped"—had a much better sense of the crowd than I did.

Charles Darwin, Gregor Mendel, Thomas Edison, Nikola Tesla, Albert Einstein, Isaac Newton, Samuel Johnson, Vincent van Gogh, Thomas Jefferson, Bertrand Russell, Jonathan Swift, Alan Turing, Paul Dirac, Glenn Gould, Steven Spielberg, and Bill Gates, among many others, are all on the rather lengthy list of famous figures who have been identified as possibly autistic or Asperger's. I do not think we can "diagnose" individuals from such a distance, so we should be cautious in making any very particular claims. Still, the possibility that some of these people are on the autism spectrum cannot be dismissed, especially once you understand autistics as being able to learn and overcome initial problems.

The economist Thomas Sowell has written two books on "late-talking children." Sowell argues that there is an entire class of people, including many people he knows and has studied, who are late talkers and have many of the traits of "mild autism." These people have very high IQs, they have strong interests in mathematics and engineering, they are sometimes introverts, they take great pleasure in their work, and they often have a special relationship to music. He has studied these people by circulating elaborate questionnaires and then collating the results. Sowell fears that these people end up misclassified as autistic and he notes that many of them are highly successful. It seems the main reason to disqualify many of them as autistic is simply that they are doing fine—they are intelligent, successful, and take pleasure in their work. Sowell is missing the point.

There is also a growing literature on children who have "recovered" from autism, often with little or no behavioral therapy. One team of researchers, led by Molly Holt, estimates that between 3 and 25 percent of children diagnosed as autistic develop to the point where they cannot be distinguished easily from non-autistic children. Deborah Fein, a psychology professor at the University of Connecticut, estimates (very roughly) a rate of 20 percent recovery. These numbers are intriguing if tentative; it is hard to know how many original diagnoses were simply wrong in the first place. But I prefer the word "learning" to "recovery"; many autistics *learn* how to overcome their cognitive disadvantages. Would we say that a non-autistic person, as he or she grows, "recovers" from having the disabilities of a four-year-old? Or would we say that the person has learned a lot?

Recognizing the power of autistic learning overturns a lot of stereotypes. There's a common belief that the "very autistic" are hopeless cases but perhaps the "mildly autistic" can meet some measure of success. That's one view, but it is a hypothesis, not a fact. We could just as easily produce another hypothesis and say that the "real autistics" are the successful people who are very consistently autistic but never diagnosed because they achieve high social status and maybe they had happy childhoods as well. They've mastered autistic styles of learning and so they have many achievements, including a good working grasp of social intelligence. Success stories don't have to be classified as cases of "mild autism"; they may well be better understood as cases of effective autistic learning.

In the field of autism research, scientific breakthroughs have come from researchers who are themselves autistic. Michelle Dawson, an autistic researcher in Montreal, insisted to her colleagues that they pursue the notion of giving the Raven's Progressive Matrices IQ test to autistics. This very different test focuses on how well an individual can complete missing segments in abstract patterns. It was once a common presumption that autistics are of lower-than-average intelligence, even if we just look at those who are not mentally retarded. This result was obtained from Wechsler IQ tests, which involve accumulated knowledge, such as command of vocabulary, or knowledge taken from everyday life, such as what might be found in a kitchen cupboard. Those are not always autistic strengths. That means autistics, unlike many non-autistics, will do much better on some IQ tests than others. When the results of some recent Raven's Progressive Matrices IQ tests were tallied, the autistics did very well indeed. In fact two of the subjects rose from the "mentally retarded" range to the ninety-fifth percentile, close to the very top.

Michelle Dawson is a researcher and an autistic but just a little more than ten years ago she was a Canadian mail carrier with no more than a high school degree. Dawson was then covered in a documentary on autism and thereby came to meet some autism researchers. They were impressed by her intellect and understanding, and now she is part of the research team and a leading figure in autism research. She still has only a high school degree but she also has an encyclopedic knowledge and understanding of the field of autism research and she is intellectually very impressive. When growing up she had enormous difficulties learning how to speak meaningfully and she succeeded only after great effort and suffering. In another era, or perhaps even today, she might have been institutionalized, but Michelle Dawson is living proof of the cognitive strengths of autism. Note that by most standards she would count as "very autistic" rather than as "mildly autistic." It seems that Hans Asperger himself—a very innovative researcher—was in some way autistic.

What is science itself but another means of mental ordering?

Neuroscientist Matthew Belmonte (who has an autistic brother) wrote: "Now as I look back I see both science and autism are compulsions to order, which differ only in their degrees of abstraction. I now feel that the same set of genetic biases that gave my brother autism gave me just enough of a desperation for order to make me a scientist, and indeed, a student of autism—enough to be driven by the same sense of impending chaos that drives my brother; yet I'm not as overwhelmed by it. I often consider how similar he and I are, and how I so easily could have been him, or he me."

I have wondered about Peter Mark Roget, the man behind *Roget's Thesaurus*. A recent biography of Roget, written by Joshua Kendall, is appropriately entitled *The Man Who Made Lists*. In the second paragraph of the book we learn that Roget was a polymath and also a chess whiz. Kendall writes: "The boyhood interest in geometry and algebra was no passing fancy . . . In some respects, mathematics proved even more alluring to Roget than verbal communication because he saw it as a pure form of language, one that addresses directly the relationships between abstract concepts." By the way, Roget also invented the log-log scale, which increased the utility of slide rules. And he wrote a 250,000-word book—his Bridgewater Treatise—on how to organize the animate world into different categories.

Here is an even more explicit passage from the biography of Roget, and I can only wonder why the concept of autism did not occur to the author: "While most children acquaint themselves with animals and plants by using all their senses—by looking, listening, sniffing, and touching—and by accessing their emotions, Peter, by contrast, relied exclusively on his mind. With neither parent available to help him process all the potentially confusing and frightening stimuli . . . Peter was forced to limit how much of the external environment he took in. Rather than experiencing the contents of the world in all their wonder, he took a shortcut powered by his keen intellect: he classified them." Peter's son John, by the way, also was described as a "classifying and arranging machine."

If you enjoy focused and sometimes repetitive activity geared toward mental ordering, these days you might fit right into the world of high achievers. I was reading the recent biography of Warren Buffett called *Snowball: Warren Buffett and the Business of Life*. From it I learned that Buffett has long had a slight obsession with trains, I learned that he loves collecting, and I learned that "he could have spent decades toiling over tables of mortality statistics, handicapping people's life expectancies. Besides the obvious ways this suited his personality—which tended toward specialization, relished memorizing, collecting, and manipulating numbers, and preferred solitude—working as a life actuary would have let him spend his time pondering one of his two favorite preoccupations: life expectancy." The point is not to claim that Buffett is autistic, as I cannot know. Instead the point is to realize that, in today's world, many autistics will be capable of high achievement, drawing of course on autistic cognitive strengths.

So far I have focused on cognition. But as listed near the beginning of this chapter, a second concept of autism (and associated notions, such as Asperger's) discusses it in terms of some mix of *personality traits* and *overt behavior*. This is the most common usage for these words but it is distinct from the understanding of the autism spectrum in terms of cognition.

It is easy to see why the personality-based and behavior-based concepts are so popular. We love to talk about other human beings and their personalities and behaviors, and so when we talk about autism we often turn our attention in the same directions. We like to use examples and point to particular traits that can be observed by others. Most of what you see or read in the media reinforces the personality-based and behavior-based views, in part because they are easy to report and turn into a human interest story. It's then easy to talk that story up to your friends and family. But a lot of these characteristics are informal generalizations with varying and uncertain degrees of truth.

The list of traits observed in autistic people—to varying degrees—includes introversion, lack of direct eye contact or unusual eye contact patterns, love of repetitive routines, self-stimulation or "stimming" (usually a repetitive body movement), a relatively flat tone of voice, a direct manner of speech, dislike of speaking on the phone, a tendency to refer to oneself in the third person, perseveration about preferred topics, and picky or restricted eating habits. There are also behavioral patterns found only in a minority of autistics but found in autistics at higher than normal rates. This includes self-injury and echolalia, or the tendency to repeat back sounds and phrases heard from other people.

That's an interesting list of characteristics, but many of the personality traits associated with autism are plain, flat-out wrong.

One common misconception is that autistics have no sense of humor. It is probably true that autistics, on the whole, have different senses of humor, so of course to some people this will appear like no sense of humor at all.

Another misconception is that autistics have no need to share their experiences or thoughts with other people. More often the method of sharing simply is different. Autistics are more likely to exchange analysis, factual information, enthusiasm for hobbies, and just plain feelings than to make typical small talk. If you engage an autistic person in an area of preferred interest, you may hear a great deal about the topic, and when autistics communicate with each other they commonly talk or write about how it feels to be an autistic in a largely non-autistic world. Nor are autistics opposed to socializing, even though many autistics lack the cognitive tools to succeed at socializing in mainstream settings. Many autistics have a hunger for contact with others, often mixed in with apprehension and fear of inadequacy. Dr. Sandi Chapman expressed an all-too-little-known point when she wrote: "As we've met hundreds of individuals with autism, almost everyone said the thing they long for the most is one good friend, or one lasting relationship . . ."

The most pernicious mistake is the belief that autistics have no sympathy for other human beings and their sufferings. Again, these mischaracterizations stem from people, sometimes even scientists, who cannot see that autistics often do or perceive things in very different ways. It is true that autistics often will not understand when other people (especially the non-autistic) are suffering but this is again a cognitive problem. It is distinct from a lack of concern or heartlessness. It's more accurate to think of autistics as coming from a different culture of sorts and simply not understanding all of the distress signals of other people, and perhaps not being able to show that they care in a way that others understand or appreciate.

It's a bit like how you might not understand when a Japanese person is trying to tell you "no" but is making the point in a different and less direct way than you are used to. When we adjust for difficulties of communication and perception in experiments, by making it clear when suffering is going on or not, it turns out that autistic people have as much compassion as do non-autistics.

Jim Sinclair, a web writer who describes himself as autistic, put it this way: "But I *do* mind when in spite of so much effort I still miss cues, and someone who has much better inherent communication ability than I do but who has not even taken a close enough look at my perspective to notice the enormity of the chasm between us tells me that my failure to understand is because *I* lack empathy. If I know that I do not understand people and I devote all this energy and effort to figuring them out, do I have more or less empathy than people who not only do not understand me, but who do not even notice that they do not understand me?"

Jason Seneca, who self-describes as Asperger's, writes:

> I have personally been accused of being cold, shallow, selfish, insensitive, egotistical, repressed, emotionally dead, incapable of emotion, and incapable of love . . . If you're like me, these accusations tend [to] come as a shock. You know that you are a sensitive and caring person; you can see these tendencies in yourself and can identify their outward manifestations. How could you be perceived so harshly?

I'd go out on a limb and suggest that autistics probably have more sympathy for the sufferings of the non-autistic than vice versa. As human beings we are all programmed to have lots of sympathy for in-group members and often not so much sympathy for anyone else. Minority groups, non-powerful groups, and "different" people are more likely to be the targets of this human failing than they are likely to be the perpetrators. The minority group is used to trying to understand the majority (even if they sometimes fail), but usually the majority has relatively little experience with trying to comprehend the feelings of the minority. The reality is that autistics have lots of compassion, most of all for other autistics. Is that really so surprising?

Remarkably, it is still entirely acceptable for a major newspaper or commentator to use the Asperger's or autism concept to refer to a person who is unfeeling or perhaps even contemptuous of the emotions of others. It's one thing when radio pundit Michael Savage calls the autistic a bunch of lazy fakers who need to be told to snap out of it. It's another when *The New York Times* uses the word "Asperger's" to denote callousness, as it has repeatedly allowed its writers to do. It is hard to imagine members of different ethnic or religious groups being discussed in the same terms.

You might think I am exaggerating but you can find prejudiced attitudes even in the scientific research literature, not just in the popular press or in seventh-grade classrooms. Michael L. Ganz, who teaches at the Harvard School of Public Health, published an entire essay entitled "The Costs of Autism." Nowhere does he consider whether autistic individuals have brought benefits to the human race. Can you imagine a comparable essay titled "The Costs of Native Americans"? David Bainbridge is an anatomist at Cambridge University. In 2008 he published a book with Harvard University Press on the brain; he claimed that autistics were lacking in the quality of alertness and he compared their cognitive faculties unfavorably to those of brain-damaged monkeys. The point is not to focus the blame on these particular individuals but rather that they have soaked up common ideas and attitudes, yet without having picked up any sense of revulsion or even hesitancy at such portraits.

Autism is so often seen as an emotionally "thin" personality type but I've grown to notice the very rich and "thick" emotional lives of autistics. There may be no better place to witness this than in the writings of self-described autistics, Asperger's, and "neurodiverse" on the web—on discussion forums, on blogs, in personal online journals, and in those scattered bits that pop up through Google. You will find an extraordinary set of intelligent, human, very emotional, and very compassionate writings, replete with all the brilliance and also the imperfections we have come to expect from the human spirit. In these web writings I found a world that I simply didn't know existed and this experience convinced me of the compassion within autistics.

In the online world you'll find Amanda Baggs, who cannot communicate effectively through normal talking but whose writings are sharper, smarter, and more piercing than most of what you read from Ph.D.s; search for her on YouTube for a startling lesson in the difference between spoken and written communication. Kathleen Seidel's site neurodiversity.com gives an overview of what is new (Seidel is not herself autistic) and the Asperger's LiveJournal discussion group presents a medley of different voices, with an active comments section and an especially high representation of female writers. Contrary to stereotype, the discussion on LiveJournal is almost unfailingly polite. On other sites you'll find crackpot theories that autistics are the lost descendants of Neanderthal man, concern from autistic parents about how they will raise their autistic children, and fears that autistics will be subject to future eugenics. You'll find lots of anger, lots of sharing of problems and tips, lots of consolation, and lots of bewilderment about a world that isn't always sympathetic or understanding.

In short, autistics are not a group of callous individuals who don't give a damn about others.

Again, although our neurologies can be very diverse, there is something fundamentally human that we all share. That's not just faith or moral philosophy, it is also backed up by science.

Autism is passed along genetically, though environmental triggers may play a role as well. Rates of autism concordance among identical twins are very high, over 90 percent by some estimates but at least 60 percent; so if one identical twin is autistic the other likely is too. Furthermore, rates of autism concordance among fraternal twins are not so high, probably less than 10 percent. So if autism-related genes have survived for so long in light of evolutionary pressures, maybe they carry important positive qualities, even if those qualities are not always visible. For instance mental ordering and acute perception can help you deal with the world and perhaps enhance your chances of survival; today those same qualities may make you a web innovator.

While parents of autistic children are more likely than average to lie along the autism spectrum, most autistics have non-autistic parents. The implication is that many so-called "normal" people are carrying around autism-contributing genes. A recent study showed that parents of autistic children were less likely to socialize and that those same parents were also less likely to make eye contact and more likely to read other people's intentions by watching their mouths rather than their eyes, a common autistic trait. There's also evidence that the parents of autistic children are more likely to have a cognitive bias toward the local processing of small bits of information, as we find among autistics. We're again back to the idea that autistic cognitive strengths and weaknesses pervade our world in many ways, often unobserved. One recent population study suggests that autistic traits are distributed across the entire population in a smooth and normal fashion, rather than into two distinct and clumped groups of "autistic" and "non-autistic." To put it bluntly, autism isn't just about "the other."

Another bias in autism research is toward children. Children are an especially vulnerable group and of course they usually have parents to take care of them and bring them to see doctors on a regular basis. It's also easier to sample children as a general population, mostly because of the public school system. So if you are trying to measure the overall prevalence of autism in the population, children are the obvious place to start.

Here is the catch. It seems easy to find lots of autistic children yet relatively hard, at least by the standards of common public perception, to find a comparable number of autistic adults. For instance a typical figure suggests that the United States has about 500,000 autistic children, for an incidence rate roughly in the range of 1 in 150. That would mean that the United States also has 1.5 million autistic adults. (These numbers are not exact.)

My belief is that the United States does in fact have something like (approximately) 1.5 million autistic adults.

But if there are at least one million autistic adults, and probably many more, the obvious question is this: Where are they? Who are they? Are they all locked up in mental hospitals? How often do you see "Rain Man" in the street? Some people think that there must be a very recent epidemic of autism. But the epidemiological measurements of autism frequency, if we adjust for the broadening definition of autism over time, do not seem to be rising each year by large amounts. If you read 2005's *Handbook of Autism and Pervasive Developmental Disorders,* you will find it stated pretty clearly by Eric Fombonne: "The available epidemiological evidence does not strongly support the hypothesis that the incidence of autism has increased." There are some ways you could argue for a gradual increase in the rate of autism but still there should be at least one million autistic adults in the United States.

So what is going on? The most likely answer is that you see autistics on a regular basis in the course of your ordinary life. You just don't usually notice them and they don't stand out because many of them are highly competent individuals, or maybe just moderately competent individuals, or maybe somewhat incompetent individuals. In any case a lot of these people are on the less visible part of the autism spectrum.

But all this is hard for many observers to admit. For whatever reason, autism still isn't socially respectable. The social hostility to autism is not always overt, as in schoolyard bullying, but it can take many subtle forms. Rightly or wrongly, autistics are often seen as staking out their independence from the group and from group norms. They're seen as questioning the psychological power of the leaders and bullies and indicating that they do not, within their minds, bend to the worlds created by those cliques (I'm not saying that is how autistics see themselves; more often autistics view themselves as simply being a certain way rather than staging a social rebellion). That's not popular. Mature adults are not so keen to attack or criticize the autistic per se, but very often the target will be someone who claims to be autistic and, at least in the view of the critic, doesn't merit the label.

It's as if that person is arrogating to himself or herself a freedom that isn't deserved and should not be recognized. It's as if only those who really suffer or who are really "handicapped" should have the "right" to claim that freedom; otherwise the freedom could spread very generally and that would be dangerous.

Following Vernon Smith's proclamation of his own self-diagnosis, one of my colleagues was dismissive, as if Vernon were a strange hypochondriac who had imagined an allergy to a nonexistent substance, or as if he had no right to arrogate to himself such a special status. But I know Vernon pretty well (I recruited him to the university where we work; he is now emeritus). I see him as a living, walking example of the cognitive strengths of autism.

It's becoming increasingly clear that there is considerable heterogeneity of outcomes in autism. The best scientific understanding of autism is changing, and it is changing rapidly. Even the formal diagnostic criteria for autism have been changed, broadened, and made less pejorative with each new edition of the diagnostic manuals. Autistics are aware, real live human beings, very often of high intelligence and sensitivity.

Given all that, we must choose how to talk about and how to think about autism. One choice is to keep thinking and talking about autism as if it were a plague. That means whenever an autistic person achieves something, we must make sure the categories are defined so this doesn't count as autism. The other choice is to look for an understanding and a terminology consistent with the dignity and skills of each individual. To me the answer is clear.

The anti-autistics may well win the fight to define autism in terms of impairments. But it's the substance of the ideas that matter.

No matter how autism ends up being defined, the cognitive strengths of whatever-we-call-what-it-is-that-I-am-talking-about will continue to reshape our world. I will use the word "autism" in this book because I think it provides a consistent framework for thinking about both the cognitive and the social issues.

Let's look some more at how society is changing, how self-education is changing, and how the web is evolving to change our lives. The ideas to follow are not *about* autism or the autism spectrum. They are ideas that have resulted from my quest for self-knowledge and these ideas have implications, I believe, for everyone. They are ideas about how we are thinking differently and what those thoughts might yield.

3

WHY MODERN CULTURE IS LIKE MARRIAGE, IN ALL ITS GLORY

We don't always recognize or appreciate intelligence when it appears in unusual or nontraditional forms. There is a corollary proposition, namely that, for cognitive reasons, we also tend to miss unfamiliar forms of beauty. Many of the world's majesties are hidden to us because they are hard to see from the outside looking in. But if we understand this idea of creating our own economy, we will be better suited to appreciating and also to creating beauty in today's rapidly changing culture.

I would like to consider three stylized facts about today's world and put them together into a single coherent vision. The facts are the following: Culture is much cheaper and more accessible than before; we engage in more and more cultural sampling; and many intelligent people complain about how ugly contemporary culture has become. Those may sound like separate phenomena but they can be tied together with some basic, intuitive economics. When that unified picture is complete, we will see that our modern world is just a bit more glorious than it is usually given credit for.

For this discussion, I'm using the word "culture" to refer to some commonly accepted cultural products. The short list for this concept of culture includes books, movies, music, and the visual arts, among other candidates. But the argument is quite general and it can apply to broader conceptions of culture as well. The key development is that we now have unprecedented access to small bits for our learning, entertainment, and inspiration. If we want to understand the big picture of how the world today is changing, we need to start small.

To start with the economics, the difficulty of access influences what kind of enjoyments we pursue. For instance, when it comes to romance not so many people are willing to fly across the country for a peck on the cheek. When the cost of a trip is high, usually you want to make sure it is worth your while. Otherwise why not just stay home? You might drive across town for a kiss if your town isn't too big, or if the traffic isn't too bad.

In the early nineteenth century, it was common for a classical music concert to last five or six hours. If people were walking long distances or arriving by slow coach, the trip had to be worth their while. A concert wasn't just about the music, it was an entire social occasion, involving drinking, the playing of cards, and a big night out. Today the Kennedy Center in Washington, D.C., puts on popular and free "Millennium Stage" concerts for no more than an hour. The hope, which so far has been borne out, is that enough people are nearby, or can get there quickly by cab, car, or Metro, to make the concerts a success. You go hear the music and then you head off to somewhere else.

Some people leave before the hour-long show is over so they can make a quick escape. They're busy and they have somewhere else to go.

If I'm going on a long trip to Brazil, which doesn't have many good English-language bookstores, the cost of getting another book to read can be pretty high. So maybe I'll bring *Moby-Dick* to reread or these days I'll bring my Kindle, stocked full of classics. The read will take a long time and I am sure it will be gripping, so that book is a good choice for a trip where access to further books is difficult. If I'm at home, access to books is quite easy. I'll grab a huge pile of (free) books from the public library and browse them. If the first nine picks off the shelf are no good it is no big deal; I can easily put them down and find some more, not to mention raid my spare books pile sitting in the dining room. There are five good public libraries within a twenty-minute drive of my house.

The general point is this: When access is easy, we tend to favor the short, the sweet, and the bitty. When access is difficult, we tend to look for large-scale productions, extravaganzas, and masterpieces. Through this mechanism, costs of access influence our interior lives. There are usually both "small bits" and "large bits" of culture within our grasp. High costs of access shut out the small bits—they're not worthwhile—and therefore shunt us toward the large bits. Low costs of access give us a diverse mix of small and large bits, but in relative terms, it is pretty easy to enjoy the small bits.

The current trend—as it has been running for decades—is that a lot of our culture is coming in shorter and smaller bits. The classic 1960s rock album has given way to the iTunes single. The most popular YouTube videos are usually just a few minutes long and most of the time the viewer doesn't stay for longer than the first ten seconds. The two-hour weekday lunch is losing ground even in Spain and Italy. Some radio ads are three seconds or shorter. In the last twenty-five years, virtually all print media have drastically reduced the length of their articles. *The New Yorker* and *The New York Review of Books* still run long pieces, but the most popular magazines—such as *Maxim* or the bestselling women's magazines—focus on articles of a thousand words or less. There are web links that direct the reader to five-word movie and song reviews, six-word memoirs ("Not Quite What I Was Planning"), seven-word wine reviews, fifty-word minisagas, and Napkin Fiction, which as the name indicates is written on a napkin. In Japan many of the bestselling novels are written to be read on cell phones, and as you might expect they are served up in small bits.

To be sure, not everything is shorter and more to the point. The same wealth that encourages brevity also enables very long performances and spectacles. In the German town of Halberstadt a specially built organ is playing the world's longest concert ever, designed to clock in at 639 years. This is also the age of complete boxed sets, DVD collector's editions, the longer director's cut of a movie, and the eight-year or sometimes even ten-year Ph.D. There is an increasing diversity of length, but, when it comes to what is culturally central, shortness is the basic trend. How many of us have an interest in hearing more than a brief excerpt from the world's longest concert? Morton Feldman's *String Quartet Number Two* fills five discs with splendid music but hardly anyone buys it or listens to it. I do, but, sadly, not always straight through.

So what is going on with these "small cultural bits"? What difference do they make to our inner lives?

The trend toward shorter bits of culture makes it easier to try new things. If you are taking items in bit by bit the tendency is to indulge your desire to sample. It's hard to sample if you're committed to reading a ten-volume history but easy to sample if most of your cultural experiences are short or small. Small cultural bits have never been easier to enjoy, record, store, and order, and as I have stated we have become infovores who love to try out and experience new bits of information as much as we possibly can.

The very pleasure of anticipating and trying—for its own sake—further encourages the new culture of small bits. When it comes to culture, a lot of the pleasure comes from the opening and unwrapping of the gift, so to speak. So you want to be trying new things all the time so you have something to look forward to and so you have the thrill of ongoing discovery.

One of the great appeals of blog posts is the expectation of receiving a new reward (and finishing off that reward) every single day. You can "start a new book"—albeit a very short one—pretty much on demand. You can finish it off not only in the same day but usually in the very same sitting. How's that for a feeling of accomplishment? The blogosphere, and many other forms of web consumption, keeps you interested by giving you pleasure from the process itself. The supply of these bits is replenished on a periodic basis, much like receiving the serial installments of a nineteenth-century novel but at a more rapid pace. It's an extreme version of one aspect of postmodernism—synthetic cultural construction by the consumer—accelerated by technology and the ease of cultural access.

Usually a blog will fail if the blogger doesn't post every day or at least every weekday. People don't like the idea of visiting the blog and coming away empty-handed, so to speak. It only seems like a visit to the blog is costless; in reality we get a brief pang of pain from "coming up empty." And once a blog disappoints I classify the site as a

"NO." The site is still only a click away, but for most practical purposes the cost of revisiting the site is now virtually infinite. In my emotional universe that site no longer exists for me and it holds a status lower than the proverbial needle in the haystack.

I can get some free gifts, pretty much any time I want, just by visiting the website of the *Guardian* newspaper (published in the U.K.). I don't go there every day (I don't have enough time), so usually most of the content is fresh to me. And it is well written, even if I sometimes disagree with the editorial perspective. While most of these presents are pretty small in terms of practical value, the reward center of my brain is activated and the mere prospect of getting something of value for free—at zero direct cost—shapes my behavior.

It can be said that the fundamental currency of the web is not money but rather squibs of pleasure and disappointment. That sounds pretty simple, but it's fundamental for understanding how the internet is reshaping our interior lives and in turn the content of our culture.

The squibs are one reason why so many people become addicted to email or other web-based activities. If you're an email addict, the arrival of each email brings a small jolt to the pleasure center of your brain and promises some prospect of a reward.

One list (on www.alexa.com) of the most popular websites in the United States, circa 2008, offers the following sites for the top thirteen:

1. Google

2. Yahoo!

3. MySpace

4. YouTube

5. Facebook

6. Windows Live (a search engine)

7. Wikipedia

8. Microsoft Network (MSN)

9. eBay

10. AOL

11. Blogger.com

12. Craigslist

13. Amazon

Of course these sites have important content but every one of the sites presents that content in a very particular way. The sites offer visitors a steady series of the equivalent of new Christmas presents. These sites have credibly established in advance that, if you visit the site, there will be some new gifts and presents waiting for you. Through a kind of operant conditioning, we associate those sites with pleasure and so we are usually excited about visiting them, and the good sites deliver and satisfy that expectation. You can look at the top websites in just about any country—including Kazakhstan and even Cuba—and they will follow these same basic principles of a steady supply of new bits of information and pleasure each day.

We also tend to prefer websites, and cultural media, that give us lots of little squibs of pleasure *up front*. It's common to note that on the internet everything is "just a click away," but this isn't quite true. A lot of what you want is two or three clicks away, or maybe more if the website designer wasn't well trained. "What does a click or two matter?" you might be thinking, but the number of clicks very often makes for the difference between happiness and frustration.

Sometimes it is we, as consumers, who turn larger items into smaller bits, and this provides an analogy to what is happening on the web every moment. Last year I bought a collection of five Eric Ambler mystery and espionage novels, in one volume, and ripped it into five separate, easy-to-transport pieces. I literally tore the book apart with my hands and fortunately the binding enabled each part to remain intact and readable. I've now read and discarded all of these separate "books." I did this disassembling for two reasons. First, I can travel and bring one of the novels without having to carry the whole big volume. The subtler and perhaps more embarrassing reason is that I get a kick from starting a book and I also get kick from finishing a book. I want to start and finish more books. We like arbitrary markers of progress and psychological reinforcements, so successful media for delivering culture must offer both of these.

One reader of my blog expressed a common attitude: "I am guilty of never having read *Anna Karenina,* because it's just so long. I'd much rather read two 300-page books than one 600-page book." Leaving a bookmark in the middle and claiming a partial achievement doesn't generate much of a charge. So the quest for the pleasures of starting and finishing again cause us to seek out the smaller cultural bits. For similar reasons, many other people seem to prefer reading book reviews to reading the books. The book review takes only a few minutes and by the time you are done you feel, rightly or wrongly, that you have learned something or that you are able to talk about the book. If newspapers are cutting back on their book review sections, in part it is because readers are seeking out the even shorter reviews on the web.

It's often debated who has offered the best or most seminal account of how the internet and web really work and hold our attention. Some people suggest it is Esther Dyson, while others mention Sherry Turkle or Neil Stephenson. I don't mean to take anything away from these very interesting thinkers, but I have two alternative nominations, more or less from left field, neither of whom wrote about the web at all.

It is two economists, namely Armen A. Alchian and William R. Allen, both of whom taught at UCLA in the 1960s and '70s. Alchian is an underground hero to many people in the economics profession. He published a relatively small number of articles in his career but each one was significant, especially when he wrote about the importance of information for understanding modern economies. He favored simple arguments that had an immediate intuitive appeal. Most of all he was renowned as a teacher and for not suffering fools gladly in the classroom. The use of a sloppy or ill-defined concept was certain to bring the student a stinging and intimidating rebuke. Allen, the junior partner of the two, ran the *Midnight Economist* syndicated radio show for many years.

In their 1972 textbook *University Economics* they presented a theorem that later became known, appropriately, as the Alchian and Allen Theorem. In technical language the theorem claims that if a fixed charge is added to the prices of two substitutable goods, such as high-quality apples and low-quality apples, the charge will increase the relative consumption of the higher-quality good. In less technical terms, that simply means that most people won't fly across the country for a mere peck on the cheek. If access is difficult, you bother only if a special someone or special apple makes it worth your while. When access is easy and nearly free of charge, many of the low-quality apples or small bits seem acceptable and thus they do not get filtered out.

The Alchian and Allen Theorem was far ahead of its time but neither Alchian nor Allen understood its full importance. Both their writings, and the small literature surrounding the claim, struggle to find significant real-world examples. Alchian and Allen themselves wrote of "shipping the good apples out." Their claim—which I do not accept—is that people who live far from apple orchards will eat tastier apples (though fewer apples) than people who live close to the orchard. In their view if you live far from the orchard you won't bother to pay the apple shipping cost unless you want a really fine apple. Maybe that's true but I think it's more important that the people who live near the orchards get their apples fresher and thus tastier, and so Alchian and Allen's main example does not really illustrate the workings of the theorem.

For the Alchian and Allen Theorem to apply in a simple and intuitive fashion, we need examples where the costs of access to a product fall rapidly and visibly. That's exactly what the internet has done and that is why the web and other innovations are bringing us what I call a culture of small bits. The internet has turned the Alchian and Allen Theorem from a curiosity in search of applications into a driver of our culture.

OK, so we have a culture of ever smaller and ever more numerous bits; what does this mean? The typical answer is that we are experiencing information overload and a knowledge glut. Haven't you seen all those people hooked up to BlackBerries while typing IMs, reading cell phone text messages, and eyeing the television (I won't say "watching") all at once? There is a lot of this going on.

Nonetheless, while it is easy to observe apparent overload in our busy lives, the underlying reality is subtler. The common word is "multitasking" but I would sooner point to the coherence in your mind than regard it as a jumbled or chaotic blend. The coherence lies in the fact that you are getting a steady stream of information to feed your long-run attention. No matter how disparate the topics may appear to an outside viewer, most parts of the stream relate to your passions, your interests, your affiliations, and how it all hangs together. At its core it's all about *you* and that is indeed a favorite topic for many people. Now, more than ever, you can assemble and manipulate bits of information from the outside world and relate them back to your personal concerns.

My daily self-assembly of synthetic experiences usually involves music, reading, and periodic glances at the web, with an email check every five minutes or so. Given how much I enjoy music, I don't like to add TV to the blend, unless it is a show I can glance at, and care about, with the sound turned off. That pretty much boils down to the NBA playoffs. Note that often I *don't* want to pick apart those distinct modes of interacting with the world and focus on them one at a time for extended hours. I *like* the blend I am assembling for myself and I like how much I learn from it.

I think of my blend as one very good way of absorbing information from the outside world, but it would be a mistake to elevate the informational purposes of the blend (however important) over the emotional import and the sense of connection. Most of all I think of my blend as an assembled set of stories and an assembled set of information packages. The blend is about the writers I read, the public figures I read about, broader intellectual narratives about the world, and indirectly stories about my own self-discovery. To me the blend offers the ultimate in interest and suspense. Call me an addict if you wish, but if I am torn away from these stories for even a day I am keen to get back to "the next episode," so to speak.

A lot of critics charge that multitasking makes us less efficient; I've read that periodically checking your email lowers your cognitive performance to the level of the inebriated. If these claims were true in general, multitasking would disappear pretty rapidly as a way of getting things done. When it comes to enjoying and assembling small cultural bits, multitasking is remarkably efficient. It is very often a *dominant* method of (interior) production and of course that is why it is so popular. The emotional power of our personal blends is potent, and they make work, and learning, a lot more fun. Multitasking is, in part, a strategy to keep ourselves interested.

If you look at measured IQ scores, they are rising over time, with each generation, in a phenomenon known as the Flynn Effect. There is no particular reason to believe that multitasking is driving this phenomenon but this does belie the common impression that people are getting more stupid or less attentive over time. Contrary to a lot of the complaints you might hear, a harried, multitasking society seems perfectly compatible with lots of innovation, lots of high achievers, and lots of high IQ scores. There are also plenty of lab experiments that show that distracting people lowers the capacity of their working memory and thus lowers their capacity for intelligent decision-making. It's much harder to show that multitasking, when it results from the choices and control of the individual, is doing us cognitive harm. Individuals can learn to improve their productivity at multitasking and task-switching, and that is exactly what is happening today.

The charge of lower attention spans has been leveled across the ages at most new cultural media—at the novel (in the eighteenth century), at the comic book, at rock and roll, and at television. Note that there has never been a "golden age" of long and earnest attention spans. Recently intellectual activity has moved onto the web—thus jumping media—at a rate that is unprecedented in human history. This is because, quite simply, the web is such a good medium for storing, communicating, and manipulating information and the end result is that we are paying more attention to information. It is easy enough to find examples where we leap from one bit of information to another, but the more important result is that information holds a stronger place in public consciousness. Information is also far more readily available to the scientific community.

Sometimes we can access and absorb information more quickly and as a result we may look less patient. But still we're putting more thought into broad ideas about society, politics, and philosophy. If you use Google to look something up in two seconds, rather than spending five minutes searching through an encyclopedia, that doesn't mean you are less patient. In fact you'll have more time for some of your longer-term endeavors, whether it be writing a treatise, cultivating your garden, or creating your own economy.

Our cultural focus on small bits doesn't mean we are neglecting the larger picture. Rather, small bits are building blocks for seeing and understanding some larger trends and narratives. The stereotypical web activity is not to visit a gardening blog one day, visit a Manolo shoes blog the next day, and never return to either. Most online activity, or at least the kinds that persist, is investment in sustained, long-running narratives. That is where the suspense comes from and that is why the internet so holds our attention.

Nicholas Carr, in a 2008 article in *The Atlantic,* asked, "Is Google making us stupid?" and basically he answered that yes, Google is making us stupid. He argued that internet culture shortens our attention spans and renders us less likely to think deep thoughts. But he missed how people can construct wisdom—and long-term dramatic interest in their own self-education—from accumulating, collecting, and ordering small bits of information. What we're growing impatient with is bits that are fed to us and that we do not really want.

Contrary to Carr, we still have a long attention span when it comes to the broader picture, and if anything Google *lengthens* our attention span by allowing us to follow the same story over many years' time. For instance if I wish to know what is new with my favorite athlete, or for that matter with a favorite economist, or if I wish to know how the debates on global warming are going, Google gets me there quickly. Formerly I needed ongoing personal involvement to follow a story for years but now I can follow long-running stories quite easily and at a greater distance. Sometimes it does appear I am impatient in discarding a book that twenty years ago I might have finished. But once I put down the book, usually I am turning my attention to a long-running story that I follow on the web. If our searching is sometimes frantic or pulled in many directions, that is precisely because we care about some long-running stories so much. It could be said, a bit paradoxically, that we are impatient to return to our chosen programs of patience.

Google lengthens our attention spans in yet another way, namely by allowing greater specialization of knowledge. We don't have to spend as much time looking up various facts and we can focus on particular areas of interest, if only because general knowledge is so readily available. It's never been easier to wrap yourself up in a long-term intellectual project, yet without losing touch with the world around you.

As for information overload, it is you who chooses how much "stuff" you want to experience and how many small bits you want to put together. If you wish, you can keep information at bay as much as you need to and use Google or text a friend when you need to know something. That's not usually how it works—many of us are cramming ourselves with web experiences and we are also buffeted by a steady stream of messages. But the resulting time pressure reflects the fun of what we are doing. Our new ways of ordering our internal mental realities are very, very appealing. You have enhanced the meaning and the importance of the small cultural bits at your disposal and thus you want to grab more of them and organize more of them, and you are willing to work hard at that task, even if it means you sometimes feel harried.

The quantity of information coming our way has exploded, but so has the quality of our filters. It's not just Google and blogs. Digg lists popular news stories, based on reader votes, and Technorati helps you trace the influence of blog posts; most importantly these services will be replaced by superior competitors in the years to come. As

Clay Shirky points out, when it comes to the web there is no information overload, there is only filter failure.

The self-assembly of small cultural bits is sometimes addictive in the sense that the more of it you do, the more of it you want to do. But that kind of addiction doesn't have to be bad. Anything good in your life is probably going to have an addictive quality to it, as many people find with classical music or an appreciation of the Western classics, or for that matter a happy marriage. Shouldn't some of the best things in life get better the more you do them?

A lot of people "unplug" and take a few days off from their email, their cell phones, their BlackBerries, and their other electronic connections to the outside world. Food writer Mark Bittman wrote a *New York Times* article about his time unplugged, free of the web and all other electronic connections to the world. The funny thing is, he presented a day of being unplugged—that's right, *one day*—as if it were a major achievement. But of course he is right: Even a day can be hard to do. I find myself sneaking back to check messages and read my favorite websites, or I decide I have to perform a few simple tasks. In part that's because I feel, rightly or wrongly, that other people, whether at work or among friends and family, need me. It's also in part because I find the self-assembly of small cultural bits to be so intoxicating and exciting. It appeals to a sense of personal control and there are far more available interesting bits than before. Whether it's the latest analysis on espn.com or the web analysis of what the last episode of *Lost* really meant, I want to know what is coming next.

That we are doing more mental ordering of culture doesn't mean we have a more ordered existence overall. The dirty dishes are still in the sink. We still have lots of chaos in our lives, lots of unperformed tasks, and lots of uncompleted missions. And, oddly enough, all the ordering is one force driving the broader chaos. Ordering has become so much fun that we specialize in ordering where it is easiest and most potent. For most of us that's on the web and the multitasking is part of the resulting order, not part of the chaos. The chaos is everywhere else, most of all in your sink. Maybe the rest of our lives is seeing *less* care and attention. Don't expect that chaos to go away any time soon.

There is again a connection between how we are using the web and autistic cognitive strengths and weaknesses. It was never the case that autistics put everything in order either. Instead autistics tend to specialize in mental ordering in favorite areas, often to the neglect of other duties and tasks. The observed autistic tendency is to be either very orderly or very chaotic, depending on the sphere of life under consideration, and that is the direction that the rest of us are moving in as well. You can credit (or blame) computer technology. We've had one sector of the economy grow at a supernormal pace, namely the web, and that unbalanced growth is feeding back into our personal and emotional lives. We take advantage of productivity improvements where we find them and we let many other areas of life lie relatively fallow. For autistic lives the uneven distribution of order stems from cognitive sources; for non-autistic lives the growing imbalance in the distribution of order stems from technology, namely the immense recent growth in the productivity of the web.

A good way to understand the self-assembly of cultural bits and how it creates an ordered, synthetic mental world is by way of contrast. Consider Mozart's opera *Don Giovanni*. The music and libretto, together, express a wide gamut of human emotions, from terror to comedy to love to the sublime, and more in between. The opera represents what is most powerful about the Western canon, namely its ability to combine so much in a single work of art. The libretto, even taken on its own, is worthy of high praise but its integration with Mozart's music brought Enlightenment culture to new heights.

Today, we don't usually receive comedy, tragedy, and the sublime all in ready-to-consume, prepackaged form. As I've stated, we're more interested in this idea of assembling the bits ourselves. For all its virtues, it takes well over three hours to hear *Don Giovanni* straight through, perhaps four hours with intermission. Plus the libretto is in Italian. And if you want to see it live, a good ticket can cost hundreds of dollars plus travel costs.

So we instead pick up the cultural moods and inputs we want from disparate sources and bring them together through self-assembly. We take a joke from YouTube, a terrifying scene from a Japanese slasher movie, a melody from a three-minute iTunes purchase, and the sublime from our memories of last year's visit to the Grand Canyon, perhaps augmented through a photograph. The result is a rich and varied stream of inner experience.

If you read what many critics say about the arts of the Renaissance or the seventeenth century, it is that human creativity then had a fierceness, a resonance, a brilliance, and a strength that it has not since attained. In the seventeenth century we have Velázquez and Rubens and Rembrandt and Brueghel and Caravaggio painting, Monteverdi composing, and Shakespeare and Milton and Cervantes writing. That's an impressive lineup. It's all so strong and so real. Most of those creations are still available to us in one form or another, at least with a bit of travel or a tolerance for digital reproductions. But in reality this older culture is losing out, in relative terms, to the competition with the internet and the iPod, and thus it is losing out to assembled small bits.

Let's say that you could carry around a perfect copy of a three-dimensional realization of a Caravaggio painting (or if your tastes are more modern make it a Picasso). You would carry a small box in your pocket, and whenever you wanted, you could press a button and the box would open up into life-sized glory and show you the picture. You would bring it to all the parties you attended. The peak of the culture of the seventeenth century (or say the 1920s if you prefer Picasso) would be at your disposal.

Alternatively, let's say you could carry around in your pocket an iPhone. That gives you thousands of songs, a cell phone, access to personal photographs, YouTube, email, and web access, among many other services, not to mention all the applications that have not yet been written. You will have a strong connection to the contemporary culture of small bits. And the iPhone is itself a thing of beauty.

Most people would prefer to carry around the iPhone, and I think they are right.

This preference has led to a corresponding shift in the meaning of cultural literacy. What cultural literacy means today is not whether you can "read" all the symbols in a Rubens painting but whether you can operate an iPhone and other web-related technologies. The iPhone, if used properly, can get you to a website on Rubens as well. The question is not whether you know the classics but whether you are capable of assembling your own blend of small cultural bits. When viewed in this light, today's young people are very culturally literate indeed and in fact they are very often the cultural leaders and creators.

Outside the window, down the street, stands a Wal-Mart, a symbol of modern America. The store seems ugly and many of the goods inside it seem ugly. I am not a Wal-Mart hater, but still it doesn't compare to *Don Giovanni* or to the lovely buildings in Prague or Vienna, and so modernity has an aesthetic burden to bear. Yet internally, our lives have never been richer. Our growing preference for small cultural bits enhances our understanding of the beauty of the broader human story, even though not every part of the outside world looks so pretty. Our new internal beauties are harder for outsiders to spot than are the fantastic cathedrals of old Europe.

So to understand contemporary culture better, let's return to our analogy with romance. Remember the claim that opened this chapter, namely that most people will not fly across the country for a peck on the cheek. Yet many long-distance relationships survive, so clearly those relationships offer some very real values. If we understand the strengths and weaknesses of these relationships, we can get a little insight into where culture today is headed. Culture doesn't analogize to relationships in every way but we can observe some basic common tendencies about the distribution of intense and ordinary pleasures, respectively.

When you travel far to meet up with your loved one, you want to make every trip a grand and glorious one. Usually you don't fly from one coast to another to just "hang out" or experience "downtime." You go out to eat, you go to the theater, you make passionate love many times, and you have intense conversations rather than just sticking with the small talk. You also fight a fair amount and you feel that your normal life has been, however temporarily, robbed from you.

The problem of course is that we "expect too much" from each visit. Remember the old question "Are we having fun yet?" The quest for continual high-quality excitement is not conducive to casual downtime together, and such routines are the glue that binds relationships together in the longer run. Or in other words the high travel costs are a potent enemy of the all-important "low expectations." You'll have a lot of thrills but it is also hard to make it work. And of course a lot of the time you're not together at all. If you really love the other person you're not consistently happy even though your peak experiences are amazing.

(If you have a long-distance relationship and are looking for advice: Do something else significant on your trip to that distant rendezvous and so lower expectations for the visit. Meet another friend too, or set up some business, or give a paper at a scintillating academic conference. Yes, you will have less time with your potential beloved, but the remaining time will get you further toward where you want to be. How much time does one need to fall in love anyway?)

Now, a long-distance relationship is, in emotional terms, a bit like culture in the time of Caravaggio or Mozart. Then costs of travel and access were high, at least compared to modern times. When you did arrive it was often very exciting and indeed monumental. Sadly, the rest of the time you didn't have that much culture at all. You couldn't run to the internet and watch Haydn on YouTube. Neither radios nor record players were around. Books were expensive and hard to get. The peaks were amazing but the disappointments were great as well because you just didn't have very good or very convenient access to a lot of quality culture. Compared to today, you couldn't be as happy overall but your peak experiences could be extremely memorable, just as in the long-distance relationship.

OK, now let's consider how living together and marriage differ from a long-distance relationship, at least with regard to the peaks vs. the steady daily experience. When you are married and living in the same house, transportation and access costs are very low. Your partner is usually right there and it's very easy to see him or her. Most days are not grand events but you have lots of regular and indeed predictable interactions.

The daily progression of marriage, of course, has an ordinariness and sometimes even an ugliness that is not always present in the long-distance relationship. Not every meeting is accompanied by passionate sex or an evening out at the theater. You might not even get a home-cooked meal but rather frozen food. There are also the dirty dishes in the sink, hedges to be trimmed, chores to do, and perhaps even diapers to be changed. In other words, there are lots of little things and lots of routine. You can think of a marriage, in its own way, as being a "culture of small bits."

In my view, if you are happily married, or even somewhat happily married, your internal life will be very rich. You will take all those small bits, and in your mind and the mind of your beloved they'll be woven together in the form of a rich and deeply satisfying narrative, dirty diapers and all. It won't always look glorious on the outside but from the point of view of interiority—what you really experience—the marriage is better than the long-distance relationship. Most people, of course, would agree. The evidence from social science also seems to confirm that most people are happier when they are married.

Now to return to culture, access has indeed become easier. The internet and other technologies mean that we literally are living with our favorite creators, or at least we are living with their creations. It is no longer a distance relationship between us and our music, for instance. It is no longer hard to get books—just download them into your Kindle or Sony Reader or whatever device replaces them. Click on Amazon or any of the many online bookstores. Culture is there all the time and you can get more of it, pretty much whenever you want. You are not committed to any particular moment of culture but you are committed to your established flow and how you have tailored the daily stream of your experience.

In short, our contemporary culture has become more like marriage in the sense that we are trading in some peak experiences for a better daily state of mind. Culture has in some ways become uglier because that is how the self-assembly of small bits looks to the outside observer. But when it comes to the interior dimension, contemporary culture has become happier and more satisfying. And, ultimately, it has become nobler as well and more appreciative of the big-picture virtues of human life.

Many critics of contemporary life want our culture to remain like a long-distance relationship, with thrilling peaks, when most of us are growing into something more mature. We are treating culture like a self-assembly of small bits, and we are creating and committing ourselves to a fascinating daily brocade, much as we can make a marriage into a rich and satisfying life. We are better off for this change and it is part of a broader trend of how the production of value—including beauty, suspense, and education—is becoming increasingly interior to our minds.

4

IM, CELL PHONES, AND FACEBOOK

It's not just that we have more music, more text, more websites, and more TV for mixing our personal cultural blends. We also have new media for experiencing and expressing ourselves and for building the richness of our lives.

Marshall McLuhan asserted that "the medium is the message" and later economists Harold Innis and Leonard Dudley showed how communications media shape human lives. Over the last fifteen years the rapid advance of digital technology has accelerated this process beyond expectations. Many of us are still trying to catch up, so I intend this chapter to be a simple guide to how some of the new communications media—such as instant messaging, cell phone texting, and micro-blogging—matter for the emotional side of our lives. They matter for our personal cultural blends and they matter for how we relate to each other and how we bond with each other. Again, the intense ordering of information isn't a sterile pursuit—it's also about human connection. This reflects the "autistic insight" that the ordering of information can be a joyous activity.

McLuhan and his followers were fond of pointing out that television was a "hot" medium because of its personality and immediacy, while print was a "cool" medium because of its objectivity and distance. What's happened is that print—in the broad sense of that term—has become a hot medium too. Today, print isn't just letters on a page; by clever use of electronic delivery media, you can create more context and make your messages more personal, emotionally richer, and more evocative in subtle ways. Counterintuitively, it is the very possibility of distance through the print medium that enables small variations in the message, designed to communicate small but important variations in emotional meaning.

Let's start with instant messaging (IM), which has now moved beyond its original teenage users. IM, like cell phone texting, rose to popularity in the teen world in large part because teens were quicker to see why the new medium was important. But IM is spreading through the general population, including of course in the workplace, where it is displacing email more each day.

The very use of IM leads us into different kinds of communication. A dialog by IM is very different than one by email, even when it is the same two people "chatting."

Here's the thing: When the ordered bits are small, small changes in cost can have a big final effect on the power of the filter, namely which bits get ordered and which do not. Again, the logic here is economic. When the message is big and important and more or less indivisible, that same message will pass more or less unscathed through many different filters. For instance if you have to communicate about fifty words of fairly exact instructions as to how to take an antidote for a deadly poison, the content of the message will be roughly invariant whether you send a handwritten note, make a phone call, or post it on a web page. The key points of the message simply have to get through whatever filter you use and it is worth making the effort to communicate the required information. But when the self-assembly of small cultural bits is going on, usually no single one of those bits or even no particular group of those bits is so important to the overall stream. Each particular bit is small in value and so the nature of the filter—and thus the medium for communication—has a big influence on what gets through and what doesn't.

In a world of cheap and readily available culture, the medium matters more than ever before. It matters for how we order information and it also matters for what gets ordered. Look at it this way: When it comes to messages, you are constructing a bundle of the message itself and the means of its delivery. The cheaper the content, the more the costs and the methods of delivery matter in shaping your decisions to communicate.

You might think it is counterintuitive that a small change in technology can matter so much. IM is only slightly easier to use than email. How hard was it to send an email in the first place? Very hard, it turns out, at least in relative terms. When you send information by IM the window for conversation is already open. You don't need that extra click to open the new email window and you don't need the extra half second for it to open. It turns out that very slight difference in extra speed and convenience makes a big difference for human communication.

Even among teenagers, an email usually has at least a sentence's worth of more or less normal content. An email might invite a person to a party, recommend a movie, or maybe outline a whole business plan, albeit in brief. We even use email to make legally binding agreements.

In contrast, here's a typical IM exchange between two people, or at least part of one:

Female: lol
Female: how amusing
Male: What?=P
Female: XD
Male: Amusing? *grin*
Female: yep
Male: Why? ^^;
Female: :patpat:
Female: don't think about it
Male: . . . I'm curious.
Female: are you now?
Male: Yep.
Female: ahahaha
Female: how cute
Male: . . . *glare*
Female: *^^*
Male: Ugh.=P
Female: ^_^
Male: So annoying.
Female: who, me?
Male: Yep.
Female: hehe

Compared to a typical email, the IM bits are shorter, the language is a pidgin creole of sorts, symbols and emoticons are more common, and many more thoughts and feelings get typed into the conversation box. Of course the ability to easily stick every thought or feeling into the box means that you develop, monitor, and report more thoughts and feelings in the first place. One study of IM found that 22 percent of all transmissions are single words, or less than single words, such as when the letter "C" is used to substitute for the word "see."

It's not just about cute expressions or strengthening our friendships. IM makes the workplace more efficient. It's easier to have a rapid-fire back-and-forth, or a worker can use IM to check whether another worker is available for a productive chat. IM means that not every query has to take the form of face-to-face contact or require an email. The judicious use of IM can decrease the number of workplace interruptions.

Some of the effects of new media are unintended and also unexpected. For instance the egalitarian nature of IM redresses a gender imbalance often found in ordinary conversation. There's lots of evidence that during face-to-face talking, men interrupt women more often than women interrupt men and that women allow this to happen or perhaps sometimes even encourage it. When you're both typing IMs, the notion of interrupting no longer makes any sense; in a way *everything* is an interruption. The power to interrupt is thus much more symmetric and the technology strips males of one of their intimidating conversational advantages. In face-to-face talk, maybe it feels like only a small cost for the woman to cut off or discourage the man's interruption but very often she will not do it. A small difference in initial cost or attractiveness makes a big difference for the final outcome. If you're the kind of guy who intimidates women excessively (intentionally or otherwise), IM is the medium for you to address that imbalance. Or if you're a woman and your guy interrupts you, try to get him on IM for a dialogue.

IM is a good way to get to know somebody, usually better than email. An IM dialogue typically has many more questions than does an email. Furthermore it is rude to not respond immediately, unless you announce that you must break off the exchange. In an IM exchange, you learn very quickly whether and how well the other person can match your pace. It is information "dancing" in a way that the oh-so-slow email never can be. And who doesn't love to dance? Truly good IM conversations are like overlapping polyphonies, with swells and peaks, breaks and moments of great intensity, and also humor. It's one of the best ways of connecting with other people. It's not a corruption of culture, rather it's a cross between the emotional tie of the mambo and the intellectual connection of rapid-fire debate. It's a new canvas on which to paint stories of friendship and sharing, not to mention romance and also sex.

Those stories and meanings of course are, most of all, painted on the interior dimension of the mind and thus they are not easily visible. So it is no surprise that many people are still suspicious of the new media. But most IM users don't think twice about the importance of IM for their lives and that is because they have a strong understanding, possibly implicit, of the power and the subtlety of the medium for framing messages.

IM is in fact a pretty good metaphor for a lot of contemporary culture. Take a look at an empty IM conversation box and you will come away unimpressed. The design people don't portray the boxes in lovely colors or give them interesting shapes. They are purely functional, at least on the major IM services. You might call them ugly. But they are a medium for fascinating connections and what is interesting in an IM exchange happens between individual human minds. The resulting excitement, connection, and beauty are hard for many outside observers to see.

Technologies of instant messaging also allow you to communicate with different people at once, possibly as many as twelve or more. You can keep as many conversation boxes open as you can keep track of and you can shift from one to another by a single move of the mouse, which is quicker than opening a new email window. Unlike clicking "send" for email, the IM box is open and ready to go. So part of the beauty of IM is not just the dance but the ability to dance with many people at the same time and on a roughly equal basis.

IM vs. email isn't the only example of how small differences in communication formats can matter. Reading a document in HTML, a simpler file format, is different from reading in the richer format of PDF. HTML is more of a lowest-common-denominator medium and it is easier for searching, linking, and using Control-C to lift content. Circa early 2009, you can't read PDFs on an iPhone. It's also quicker to scroll through an HTML document, if only because you must first click in a PDF document before "page down" will work. That may seem like a tiny difference but when I see a PDF document my first instinct is to print it out or otherwise ignore it. When I see something in HTML format my first instinct is to read it. That usually leads to a big difference in final results. As the web develops, I see HTML gaining in influence over PDF. PDF is the main format for scientific research, but the reporting of that research is usually done in HTML, whether through blogs or mainstream media sites.

Just as IM differs from email, cell phone texting is very different from making a cell phone call. Having grown up with pay phones and AT&T calling cards, I used to think making a cell phone call was so simple. But once you think about it a bit, you realize it isn't so simple at all. When you make a cell phone call, you open yourself up to being asked questions. You have to commit yourself on matters of tone and also on key information, such as telling your mother where you are and what you are doing and why you didn't call earlier. A phone call is actually a pretty complicated emotional event and that is one reason why so many people remained "cell phone holdouts" for so long. A cell phone (at least if you carry it, leave it on, and answer it) means that other people can call you almost anytime they want to.

I have a growing number of friends who, even if they own and carry cell phones, avoid phone calls altogether. A phone call is a demand on you. A phone call is a chance to be rejected. And a phone call is a chance to flub your lines or overplay your hand.

With texting, the messenger or respondent is in more control. The messenger can choose when to answer the initial query and the responder can more easily limit the information sent back in response. The whole technology fits well into the idea of a life constructed from disparate cultural bits. And of course the very existence of texting (and email) makes a phone call all the more emotionally fraught. It used to be you could just call somebody up to chat; today a phone call often brings the presupposition that something is deeply wrong (or right) or perhaps you have an engagement or a death to report. Of course the greater the emotional pressure placed on phone calls, the more people will resort to substitutes for calls, including texting and also email. That makes the event of a phone call more important still. Phone call cowards will in return be even less likely to make the calls.

You might think that texting is ideally suited for the exchange of practical information, such as where and when to meet, and indeed it is. But texting also opens up emotional doors. It offers immediacy combined with a certain amount of distance. Just as people will write things in an email that they might not say out loud, so will they text feelings and revelations with greater comfort. Or if you just want to ask a question, you can be more direct without seeming rude. The medium requires directness and so it shifts the standards for polite discourse. No one expects you to beat around the proverbial bush and in this regard texted "conversations" are more like many of the conversations between autistic people. Just come right out and say what you mean.

Even though the idea of receiving or making a call is emotionally threatening to many people, carrying a cell phone is also a form of emotional comfort. Many people, especially teenagers, like the idea of carrying it all the time. It symbolizes a kind of protection, an electronic nest, and the possibility of always being in touch with friends and family, if need be. The option of texting strengthens that nest feeling while diminishing the potential threat of calls. So to make the cell phone more of a security blanket, texting should serve some emotional functions, and indeed it does. Donna and Fraser Reid have written of "'Text circles'—the idea that Texters seem to form closely knit groups of 'Textmates' with whom they engage in regular, maybe even perpetual, contact."

Texting is encouraging some forms of communication over others.

It's a very good way to communicate "I told you so" or to admit fault without setting off a long verbal argument.

Japanese teens and lovers use cell phone texting to communicate a steady stream of emotions between their "fleshmeets." Before a date it is common to exchange numerous messages of longing during the afternoon, often peaking as the date time approaches. On the journey home, after the actual encounter, further messages are used as "fading embers of conversation" and this trail of feelings can continue for days until the next date rolls around. That's harder to manage with your tone of voice. Texting has reached its height in Japan, and you can walk around Tokyo all day and see hundreds or thousands of texters but maybe only a few people actually making a cell phone call.

You also can send and read texts during your downtime or when you're supposed to be doing something else. Or maybe you text when someone else is driving, as does my wife, and you interrupt your texting every now and then to maintain the conversation. A cell phone chat isn't as flexible across the same variety of situations.

Micro-blogging services such as Twitter, Jaiku, and Pownce also shape discourse. Most of all, micro-blogging cultivates our sense of the importance of the small bit.

In case you don't already know, micro-blogging allows you to post short observations only. In other words, sites limit the number of characters in a single unformatted blog post. In the case of Twitter, currently the best-known of these services, the maximum is 140 characters and the message is put in a small cloud up on blank empty space. If it's small bits you want—for the reasons discussed in chapter 3—Twitter is one way to make sure that is what you get. Think of Twitter and related services as sending you very short updates about the people you care for or from the people who best supply you with new information.

A typical Twitter post, or "tweet" as it is called, might simply read:

Trying to do better

Some other favorite tweets I have read or read about are:

Brief nap gives me a second chance to wake up on the wrong side of the bed

Our Safeway is like The Island of Misfit Toys, but for groceries

Contemplating going to see Transformers by myself. Could anything be geekier?

when twitter first started, we twittered about things other than twitter, right? RIGHT? restore my faith in humanity!

And finally:

Do you have a Twitter strategy? Scoble says you need one and a Facebook strategy too. Scrambling to get one of each LOL!

I'm not sure you're all so impressed but of course those tweets weren't intended for you anyway. A tweet makes the most sense within a context, a friendship, and an ongoing conversation, if only on Twitter. By the way, if you meet with a tweet reader, it is called a tweetup. And in case you didn't know, it's easy to have your friends' tweets delivered directly to your cell phone in the form of text messages.

The Twitter page is unpretentious, to say the least, and even a technophobe can learn how to do it in seconds. If you know more you can customize the background to look pretty, but perhaps plain is more to the point. Most users now post directly, without visiting the page at all.

Why would anyone ever want to Twitter, given that we already have email, blogs, cell phones, IM, and good old-fashioned speech, not to mention the handwritten postcard? Micro-blogging is unique. The pressure on the content is defused deliberately. It's *supposed* to be content that you wouldn't bother sharing with most people. Tweets are supposed to be extremely ordinary and everything about the medium pushes you in that direction. Twitter allows you to build intimacy with one group of people but not another, or in other words you can reach out and build intimacy with the people who are interested in you no matter what. Or sometimes a reader—a perfect stranger—may want to see what your shortest thoughts are really like; maybe it's a kind of test of how interesting you really are. Traditional blogging, in contrast, uses longer posts. This form of blogging interests mostly those people who like writing for its stand-alone, paragraph-long merit. That's all fine and good, but it's not the most effective tool for developing a friendship, or for that matter an obsession.

Micro-blogging fills in the gaps. Too often I've had a periodic conversation with a friend or family member and been reduced to reciting the latest "news," as if it were a series of bullet headlines. Micro-blogging recognizes that the ordinary fabric of daily life— the small bits of existence—is a big part of "what's new." Rather than being impersonal, it brings people together. If someone is reading your tweets and they ask "What's new?" all of a sudden the conversation can take place in a thicker and richer context. The conversation can be emotional and evocative rather than sounding like CNN. It's another example of how mastering some small bits can give you a richer, bigger perspective on the world.

There's even a service called Twist (twist.flaptor.com/?tz=-5) that tracks trends on Twitter. Twitter posts about being drunk, not surprisingly, peak on Friday and Saturday nights, and twittering about hangovers peaks the following mornings. The days of the week that get the most mention are Friday, Saturday, Sunday, and Monday, thereby illustrating the centrality of the weekend in our interior lives.

But it's not just about parties. If you're micro-blogging all the time, you are forced to be more philosophical about what you are doing. *Which* little event from today is the one I want to list? And how should I describe it? What about the event was really important? Those may sound like stupid questions but micro-blogging is making many of us more contemplative and more thoughtful.

It would be easy for the Twitter site to allow more characters in a single tweet and thus more content, but that would, as they say, ruin everything. Twitter has branded itself as specializing in a very particular style of blogging, namely short status updates on what the writer is feeling or doing. It wouldn't cost you much time to put your longer ideas in the form of successive tweets, but even the very slight annoyance of starting a new tweet usually stops that from happening. No one is out there trying to write an epic poem through successive tweeting and indeed the content on Twitter is almost exclusively of the short variety.

Twitter differs from email in another important way as well. An email is pushed into your face, whether you want to read it then or not. While you might say "I can always wait," the reality is that most of us feel the pressure of an accumulating in-box. Twitter you visit when you want and stay there for as long as you wish to. It's demand-driven and the pace is under your control. You don't have to pretend you are listening. Nor does anyone assume that you must have read his or her tweet, so it is OK if you stay away altogether. "What, you didn't get my email!?" is not an issue in this medium. J. P. Rangaswami has described Twitter as more like a side-to-side conversation, like you might have casually in a bar with a stranger, rather than a face-to-face conversation over the dinner table or an office desk.

As I discussed in chapter 1, how much people enjoy reality, and *how* people enjoy reality, depends on how they order it in their minds. By ordering material you create the surrounding frames. Standard behavioral economics views "framing effects" as distorting our decisions, but in many circumstances framing effects help make our lives real, vivid, and meaningful, just as Twittering can make our smallest choices more salient.

We choose to send or receive messages in particular ways, in part, to determine which kinds of framing effects will influence our thoughts and emotions. The greater the number of media we have to choose from, the more likely this process will suit our tastes. Human behavior still will be influenced by behavioral "distortions," but there is a better way to think about how those distortions operate. To trace and understand your behavioral mistakes, do not focus on the cognitive distortions occasioned by any single, given instance of framing, especially as it might be measured in a laboratory setting. The framing you encounter in the real world usually represents your choice and you have some reason for it. In other words, most behavioral studies of framing effects eliminate competition—in this case competition between messages—one of the most fundamental features of a market economy. You probably made that irrational decision because it fits with the way you have chosen to frame your reality, and in turn your own economy, and thus you had some reasons for that framing, even if it wasn't the very best decision of all those available.

The better way to understand human imperfections is to focus on what I call an überdistortion, namely that we, when selecting from a broad menu of options, don't always make the right choice of framing effects. In other words, if you want to make better decisions, you should be more self-reflective about how you are choosing to frame the messages you send and receive. You should think more about who you listen to and who you read.

Let's consider an example. Frederic Brochet, a psychologist at the University of Bordeaux, ran some experiments to test experienced wine tasters. He invited fifty-four wine experts to give their sensory impressions of a red wine and a white wine. He was told that the red wine tasted of "crushed red fruit," among other traditional descriptive responses. He was told that the white wine tasted of lemon, peaches, and honey, all traditional white wine flavors. The experts then returned for another tasting, but this time the white wine was dyed red with (tasteless) food coloring. The same experts described the same white wine, only now it looked red. All of a sudden those experts found flavors in the white that usually they ascribed to reds. What used to taste like lemon, peaches, and honey now tasted like black currants. These experts had no reason to lie and in fact their answers subsequently caused them embarrassment. Their blather about the wines was sincere.

That's a neat experiment, but it's wrong to focus too much on the conclusion that people are excessively tricked by the pronouncements of authority. The experiment itself preordained that the wine tasters heard a positive message about the wine. In the real world, wine tasters choose the sources for their information and framing. Some of those sources (e.g., wine magazines) will "talk up" the quality of the wine experience while other sources (Budweiser, or the temperance league) will talk down the quality. To figure out the net bias, the question is which sources are overselected or underselected. Maybe the wine magazines receive more attention than the temperance league, but the effect of the magazines is not just a rude trick. The wine magazines offered a preferred means of framing aimed at helping us appreciate expensive wine, whether by learning, placebo, or, as is usually the case, some mix of both.

There are cases when we *want* to be tricked by our messengers, even though we don't quite want to describe the process to ourselves in those terms. The more expensive wine really can taste better, simply because it is more expensive, and we want to keep that as one of our pleasures in life. It's what helps to make "special occasions" feel so special, namely that we went to considerable trouble to do something. In part our expectations *make* the difference a real one through a kind of placebo effect. But if we have chosen that placebo effect, such a "trick" can bring real human benefits. Dan Ariely did a famous study where he showed that more expensive pain relief medication, even of similar quality, does a better job at alleviating pain. Or maybe I love my wife more because I had to court her with great passion. These are often opportunities rather than problems.

These results, by the way, aren't all new and revolutionary but rather they reflect some age-old wisdom. Adam Smith, in his 1759 book on moral psychology, *The Theory of Moral Sentiments*, suggested that we enjoy and value an experience more if it took more self-command and more sacrifice to bring it about. The cost of getting something helps us frame it as something important. This is also a theme in the writings of the Roman Stoics, who were a major influence on Smith.

(These results make you wonder. Should we tell patients that the cost of their hospital treatment was really high? Can we reap more of the benefits of placebos without deceiving people? Is this one reason why top restaurants don't hand out reservations so easily, namely so that the food tastes better when people go through trouble to get in? Is this why some women play "hard to get"?)

Studies of framing effects have been done on red wine and pain relief tablets but not on Facebook or iPods; for one thing those services are too new to have received comparable attention and also the outcomes from those services are harder to measure. But I wish to suggest that framing and expectations still shape the final results, in this case the human relationship. Facebook, by organizing your friends in a new and fun way, actually influences your friendships. Not just because those people are easier to contact, or for other practical reasons, but because they take on greater importance in your mind. When you "friend someone" (that is Facebook lingo for asking to connect to their page as a "friend") you then expect the relationship to be a more intimate one than it had been and so this expectation is affirmed by both parties. You are more likely to think of that person as your friend, and indeed you are more likely to think of yourself as a friendly person. Both expectations will—on average if not in every case—become self-fulfilling prophecies. It's like how you talk yourself into thinking that the more expensive wine has a more profound taste simply because it is supposed to.

I joined Facebook in part because I wanted to learn how it works. I didn't have any "felt need" for the service, although I quickly found I enjoyed it and started using it for its own sake. Ever since I mentioned Facebook on my blog, hundreds of people have friended me unilaterally. I friended them all back, without exception. Every now and then I meet one of them. And you know what—when I meet one of them, *they really do feel like my friends.* Not good friends or close friends, so maybe the word "acquaintance" would be better (though they can't call it "Acquaintancebook"). But I approach them with a warmer glow than otherwise, simply because they "friended me." If an actual *friend* has friended me on Facebook, so much the better. Facebook has made me friendlier. Call that superficial if you want, but it is a better feeling than continued indifference or neglect. It is a framing effect that I have chosen to keep, and to my advantage.

It is less clear, however, that Facebook expands our friendliness in every regard. Facebook also makes friendship a little too easy and you will recall from above that a feeling of sacrifice sometimes makes us appreciate something more. Facebook gives us a lot of friends or acquaintances. Friendship becomes a bit less like that precious, hard-to-find diamond. But rest assured, Facebook is not destroying all ideals of tight and eternal friendship. If you have a truly close friend from, say, high school, Facebook makes it easier to stay in touch with that person's life. That ease means you may in some ways value the general phenomenon of friendship less, but your best friendships will be stronger, closer, and based on more regular contact.

The inflating away of the friendship concept is not inevitable in a networked world. If you wish, you can have another social networking service, more exclusive in nature, reserved for those who are your true, lifelong friends. You can follow only your five dearest friends on Twitter or send text messages to only your immediate family. Facebook isn't the only framing device out there and you can direct your attention elsewhere to offset any unwanted biases of Facebook. Framing effects are not just one-off influences but rather we choose them from a broad portfolio of options. We mix and match framing effects as we see fit, and so it is again a mistake to focus on the cognitive biases uncovered in stand-alone experiments under lab conditions. If there is any important bias in human affairs, it is again the überbias of choosing which framing effects to enjoy. When it comes to friendship, I'm not so worried that people will choose the framing effects that make all their close friends go away. Again, a networked world is very often an intimate world.

I once met a guy who had so many "friending" services (it seemed he had as many services as some people have friends) that he constructed an entire web page to organize them. He understood that each social network service performs a slightly different function in terms of how it brings people together and what kinds of ties it produces. The deliberately impersonal nature of LinkedIn, for instance, is part of its business and professional image; that same strategy could not work for Facebook. It's again a case where competition really helps us produce exactly the right kind of human tie for each circumstance.

By this point the philosophical questions probably have occurred to you. How do these framing effects really work? Does Facebook actually make your friends more valuable? Or does it just make them *seem* more valuable? Is the time spent with them actually any better? Or do we just remember that time more fondly because we gaze on the photos afterward, on the Facebook site? Or maybe the time together isn't any better, but perhaps you anticipate it in some fun way, such as by exchanging plans to meet over Facebook or IM. Which feelings are the reality and which are the illusion? Is Facebook just a "friends placebo" in lieu of the real thing?

I'm not sure these questions have final, absolute answers. When perceptions shape reality, and vice versa, there's not always a simple way to separate the back-and-forth influences.

Communications media have the strongest impact on your emotions when they receive social validation, and that is exactly how the iPod, Facebook, and many other modern innovations work. Yes, you order your friends on Facebook, but this isn't a purely private act. Your friends, by visiting your page, observe your ordering, they talk about it, they analyze it, they respond with their own changes in ordering, and they confirm the realness of your ordering in your mind. You lend your iPod to your friends, not just to be the proverbial nice guy, but to let people see what music means to your life. As the world sees you as a lover of Radiohead, so you become one all the more. Religions, Alcoholics Anonymous, and terrorist cells all understand the importance of social validation to firing up and firming up people's commitments. Adam Smith knew that few men "can be satisfied with their own private consciousness" without social recognition of what they have done. This is yet another way in which Facebook boosts friendship rather than degrades it.

Amazon actually makes your books more interesting, and it makes the books you imagine you might read (but don't) more fun too. You-Tube makes your favorite TV show more memorable and more iconic. EBay turns collectibles into a greater source of pride. The behavior of your avatar in Second Life will shape your skills and attitudes in your first life. In other words, the techniques of ordering are spilling over into the very content and enjoyment of our culture and our lives. It reminds me of the Borges short story "Tlön, Uqbar, Orbis Tertius," which is based on the idea of an obsessive ordering of the world through a fanciful encyclopedia. At some point the mythical objects of the encyclopedia world seep into reality and the principles of ordering start to govern and shape real-world events.

RSS readers are increasingly common. RSS stands for Really Simple Syndication. The reader "delivers" web articles and blog posts to you in a single, consolidated format; FeedDemon and Google Reader offer two well-known RSS services. In other words, if I am reading five (or fifty) blogs I don't have to visit all of the sites. I can program my reader to deliver the post—without advertisements I might add—whenever something new is published on that site. That sounds pretty neat, right? Well, I'll tell you this. Once you decide to add five, ten, or maybe two hundred people to your RSS feed, those become the important thinkers and writers for you. They achieve a salience as the people you have certified as sufficiently worthy to have delivered to your (figurative) doorstep. It's different from visiting a blog every now and then. In a very discrete and distinct way, you have framed those people as "worth reading on a regular basis" and their careers and influence will benefit from that framing for a long time to come. You, as a reader, are likely to trust them more than you used to.

The web also makes it easier for us to focus on our points of similarity with others. For instance there is the well-known phenomenon of the "Googletwin" or the "Googlegänger," patterned after the German word "Doppelgänger," which refers to your ghostly double. A Googlegänger is a person who shares your exact name and appears in your Google searches. Of course whenever you Google yourself, you learn about the doings of that namesake person as well.

It turns out that many people have strange attractions to others with the same name. One writer, named Angela Shelton, tracked down and met forty other Angela Sheltons; she relates her experiences in a book titled, unsurprisingly, *Finding Angela Shelton*. The website HowManyAsMe lets you find how many others have your name, Facebook coalitions are organized around common names, and there is a group trying to establish a world record by gathering together more than 1,224 people named Mohammed Hassan. There was a nine-year-old Tyler Cowen in a soccer league somewhere and every now and then I wonder how he is doing.

There's evidence, from many fields of study, that people are strongly attracted to others who resemble them in terms of name or other characteristics, even accidental characteristics. Jeremy Bailenson, the director of the Virtual Human Interaction Lab at Stanford

University, describes self-similarity, as it is called, as "one of the largest driving forces of behavior of social beings." What's interesting is how strongly new web technologies bring self-similarity into our lives. We can track down these commonalities, be it our names, the high school we went to, our hobbies, our neurologies, or our favorite vacation spots.

One of the most notable features of the web is how easily we can form groups and affiliations. We can join Facebook groups, we can meet these "peers" in virtual worlds, we can chat with them, and we can email them from a distance. It is much easier for us to find people with common interests than before and it is much easier to organize and order our relationships with those people. We "tag" or "bookmark" those people rather than lose track of them. We can meet them or maintain a structured relationship at a distance. By allying with "similars" in this way, we reframe and strengthen our preexisting identities and thus we become more like our true selves.

Even very unusual people can find peers through web search, chat groups, and virtual realities. These newly found similarities make it more fun to be yourself and the resulting affiliations are reinforced socially.

Cass Sunstein has argued that the web polarizes people politically for reasons like the above. We'll see, but I think the final effect will be a more tolerant and cosmopolitan one. (Keep in mind we've had the web for a while now and our recently elected president Barack Obama succeeded by running on a non-ideological platform; while partisanship will certainly return I doubt if the web is the problem.) For most people our political connections are not the major source of our identity, even if in public arguments we sometimes pretend they are. Being a Democrat, Republican, Libertarian, etc. doesn't mean any single thing for what we are actually like as human beings. One thing we do on the web is seek out others who are like us in non-political ways and then we cement those alliances and friendships. Over time, we will discover that many of these truly similar people do not in fact share our political views. Then we realize that politics isn't as important as we used to think.

The nature of the web will favor some commonalities over others. Specifically it favors commonalities that can be spelled out in very exact, searchable language. For instance if you meet a group of people in person, it might be possible to construct a small coalition of members who are whimsical in a very particular yet hard-to-describe way. You know such people when you see them and you can all go off and take a short pedal boat ride together. But constructing the same coalition with a Google search would be much more difficult. Maybe I know what notion of "whimsical" I have in mind, but I can't write it down exactly in a way that anyone else would understand. What I have in mind is "the kind of whimsical like that girl Alison Murray I used to know." I typed that into Google and really didn't get anything useful. But type in "blogs about model trains" or "Victorian collectibles" and you will be busy for the rest of the day.

The web thus encourages us to pursue our identities and alliances based around very specific and articulable interests. And do you know which group has a strong preference for specific and clearly articulable interests in the first place? That's right, autistics. This is yet another way in which the web is altering our behavior and shaping our interests in what is broadly a more autistic direction. Relative to many non-autistics, autistics find it easy to use the web to track down what interests them. But no matter what your neurology, the web is encouraging your affiliations that are searchable and discouraging your affiliations that are not. The web is strengthening the aspects of your identity that are fact-based and easy to spell out in very direct language.

Finally, framing effects are more important than ever before. Some experiences, and some goods and services, are more subject to framing effects than others. If someone shoots you in the heart with a bullet, framing effects probably don't much matter. You're going to die, and if you survive the immediate impact it's going to be unpleasant, no matter what your attitude. If you give a hungry man food, he is going to enjoy it no matter how it is framed; Cicero wrote, "Hunger is the best sauce." The more visceral the experience, the less likely it is that framing effects will make a big difference for your pain or enjoyment.

This means that wealthy, secure societies offer greater scope for framing effects, and in particular they offer greater scope for beneficial framing effects. Competition gives you the chance to construct the whirlwind of influences that you most prefer. For that process to work smoothly, try to avoid the überbias of picking the wrong framing effects. Focus your wisdom on choosing the right media for your messages. If you don't like how Facebook shapes your attitudes toward your friends, avoid it or supplement it with something different or something better. Write a blog post, a cell phone text, an email, or a Tweet. When all else fails, there's still that good ol' slow-delivered, handwritten postcard.

How you decide to communicate is a fundamental choice in the creation of the most prosperous economy your life can provide.

5

THE BUDDHA AS SAVIOR
AND THE PROFESSOR AS SHAMAN

I've talked about the power of ordering information, but when it comes to being an infovore, we need to know what kinds of biases may hamper our ability to create our own economy of real internal value. Either those biases can be corrected or even if not, understanding a bias can give us a richer internal mental life.

Fortunately we don't have to start from scratch in this intellectual quest. There is already a long-standing discourse on these questions, namely within the framework of Buddhism. Buddhism of course is a religion but it also is a philosophy of human life. Some parts of Buddhism favor intense focus on small things but the doctrine is more skeptical when it comes to manipulating information and putting that information into structured orders. Buddhism too often sees those practices as harmful obsessions. What I'd like to do in this chapter is look at the Buddhist take on mental ordering (pro and con), ask what we can learn from it, and then move on to the mirror question: If Buddhism can moderate some of our more extreme desires for mental ordering, what is a useful tool for correcting a *deficit* of mental ordering? The answers point in some surprising directions.

It is difficult to make general proclamations about Buddhism as a whole. It is practiced, or believed, in varying degrees, by more than a billion people. It exists in multiple and sometimes varying schools of thought, including the Theravada Buddhism of Southeast Asia, the Vajrayana Buddhism of Tibet, and the Zen Buddhism of Japan, just to name a few approaches. There is no single canonical text or statement of Buddhist doctrine. Most versions of Buddhism stress the primacy of practice and the attainment of wisdom through Buddhist ways rather than through reading; I never have been a practicing Buddhist so that limits my understanding. It is possible to debate whether Buddhism is a religion at all; maybe it is a philosophy of life, a philosophy of mind, or just a way of being.

But despite that complexity, it is possible to look at Buddhism and extract some consistent threads that add up to a critique of mental ordering. Don't think of my points as a once-and-for-all description of Buddhism with a capital "B" but rather as a kind of collation, relevant for the question of bias at hand but theologically speaking not standing on its own two feet.

Buddhism is most sympathetic to mental ordering, and to the practices of many autistics, when it promotes the notion of focus on a small object. For instance the Dalai Lama once wrote a book called *The Universe in a Single Atom*. This title accords with the more general Buddhist view that small parts of the universe contain great wisdom and beauty, if only we train our minds to find the right kind of access.

With *The Universe in a Single Atom* in mind, consider the account of Sue Rubin, a highly intelligent autistic woman. She writes: "Although not extremely productive, I like to spend parts of my day listening to music and playing in the sink. As trivial an activity as that may sound, I stand in front of the sink and play with the water. Nothing else is on my mind but what is in front of me. School, home life and family escape my mind for that brief moment . . . I use the time in front of the sink as an outlet during crowded times. It is a relaxation tool that I can too tear myself away from."

Sue also reports having an infatuation with spoons, for related reasons, and I have read or heard similar accounts from many other autistics, albeit with varying objects. It's not just about relaxation but such focus is also a means of long-run cognition. It is a way of approaching the day's problems afresh and with a new perspective. In these regards, autistics are the culmination of Buddhist thought and indeed Buddhist practice, even though few of them are following Buddhism in any deliberate sense. Oddly we call these tendencies glorious when they are affiliated with Eastern religion but we call them pathological, or we think of them as just plain weird, when they are performed by autistics. I genuinely wonder why we do not accord Sue Rubin the same respect that we grant the Dalai Lama. He's had to work very hard at what she can do quite naturally and skillfully.

It's not just about autistics and Buddhists. Few people care to think about their own cultural interests as being like Sue Rubin's spoons, but when you look at the fundamentals it is not obvious that there is a categorical difference. Is enjoying the sound of music, or appreciating the texture of a painting, such a fundamentally different enterprise than enjoying a plastic spoon? You can tell all sorts of stories about how the song or the painting is embedded in a cultural and historical context and rich with deep additional meaning, but I'm not sure whether this cuts for or against the methods of Sue Rubin. You can think of many autistics as simply bypassing traditional cultural canons—which they do not need—and going to a more direct perception of the underlying aesthetic values.

In spite of some similarities, the potential alliance between Buddhism and autism goes only so far. For one thing, autistics tend to have strongly preferred objects for such acts of contemplation and cognition. For Sue Rubin a plastic spoon has a special status—for whatever reason—that most other objects do not approach. Buddhist philosophy is broadly suspicious of such particular attachments. I believe one factor behind the difference in perspective is that autistics have a preferred method of mentally ordering the different "spoon experiences"—and thus other objects will not do—but that remains my speculation.

Most fundamentally, Buddhist philosophy is suspicious of complex forms of mental ordering and that is where Buddhism parts company with autism and also parts company with how our (nonautistic) lives are changing. Buddhism has a tendency to view reason, in the Western sense of that term, as engaged in separating, classifying, discriminating, and ordering to an extreme and sometimes oppressive degree. These processes of reasoning may help us see or understand the parts but they distract our attention from the perception of all-important "wholeness." Ordering also represents a kind of mental ownership or possession and in that sense it is constraining rather than liberating according to Buddhism. Our mental investment in what we have ordered keeps us from maximum harmony and freedom.

Buddhism also encourages the practice of meditating on emptiness, and it is hard to impose an interesting order on emptiness. "Om" doesn't have the same stacking and ordering opportunities as does, say, your Twitter account, or for that matter a set of plastic spoons. Indeed the difficulty of ordering emptiness is part of the point of the Buddhist approach. The use of a mantra, a very simple sound that is uttered or imagined repeatedly, limits the ordering possibilities by filling the mind with something homogenous and difficult to structure. The mantra is a kind of net or handcuffs to be placed on the mind.

The general Buddhist emphasis is on developing what is called mindfulness. The concept of mindfulness refers to awareness of one's own thoughts and actions in a serene and whole-embracing manner. We should be aware of what is around us, and its profundity, and we should not be distracted by the patterns and orders we may seek to impose on that reality. Mindfulness comes from extensive practice and the shedding of bad mental habits; Western reason, ordering, and classification are seen as potential enemies of mindfulness and that again sets up Buddhism as a foil to our mental excesses. It is easy to imagine a Buddhist recommendation to take a walk in the forest. It is harder to imagine a Buddhist recommendation to intensively edit a Wikipedia page.

I've found some of these ideas to crop up especially frequently in the Zen Buddhism of Japan but they are amenable to Buddhist thought more generally. It may sound odd to juxtapose Buddhism and neurology, but many Buddhists themselves insist on a connection between the two branches of human thought. The Dalai Lama for instance is widely read in neurology and he often meets with leading neurologists for an exchange of information and views. He stresses that Buddhism should be compatible with the latest scientific findings from neurology and in turn scientists come to him to hear what Buddhists have learned from the meditation practices of monks. In particular the Dalai Lama is interested in the idea of neuroplasticity, namely the malleability of the human mind with respect to repeated practice. In other words, if you practice calm enough you may in fact become calmer. Neuroscientists consult with Buddhist monks because the monks have lifelong experience in trying to mold their minds in particular ways, namely toward greater harmony and calm. It seems that many of the Buddhist meditation techniques, if applied consistently over many years' time, can reshape the mind to some extent and also give the mind greater control over the body.

To appreciate Buddhism as an antidote to the modern world, and to our growing obsession with ordering information, consider the following practices.

The late Fischer Black, the brilliant economist who helped invent options pricing theory in finance, was obsessed with recording his ideas and conversations. Perry Mehrling, Black's biographer, wrote about Black's life:

He did almost all of his work in an outlining program called ThinkTank, which he used as a kind of external associative memory to supplement his own. Everything he read, every conversation he had, every thought that occurred, everything got summarized and added to the database that swelled eventually to 20 million bytes organized in 2,000 alphabetical files . . . Reading, discussion and thinking that Fischer did outside the office was recorded on slips of paper to be entered into the database later. Reading, discussion, and thinking that took place inside the office was recorded directly. While he was on the phone, he was typing. While he was talking to you in person, he was typing. Sometimes he even typed while he was interviewing a prospective job candidate, looking at the screen not the candidate.

Ed Boyden, a blogger for *Technology Review,* does something similar to Black but with superior technology (Black passed away in 1995). He describes the technique as "conversation summaries." It is best explained by quotation:

> I find it really useful to write and draw while talking with someone, composing **conversation summaries** on pieces of paper or pages of notepads. I often use plenty of color annotation to highlight salient points. At the end of the conversation, I digitally photograph the piece of paper so that I capture the entire flow of the conversation and the thoughts that emerged. The person I've conversed with usually gets to keep the original piece of paper, and the digital photograph is uploaded to my computer for keyword tagging and archiving. This way I can call up all the images, sketches, ideas, references, and action items from a brief note that I took during a five-minute meeting at a coffee shop years ago—at a touch, on my laptop. With 10--megapixel cameras costing just over $100, you can easily capture a dozen full pages in a single shot, in just a second.

There is a greater extreme yet. A research project called MyLife-Bits tries to record everything in your life, of course putting it into archival and searchable form. It copies every web page that is visited and every email or IM that is sent, records every phone call and every piece of music that is played or TV show that is watched. A GPS feed sends in continual information on your whereabouts and of course that information is correlated with the other captured data. All this information is stored in a well-ordered digital archive, or "e-memory." Gordon Bell, who experimented with MyLifeBits for six years, also wore a SenseCam, a camera that is programmed to take pictures in response to particular cues, such as when the infrared sensors detect a warm body nearby. If the level of light changes significantly, the camera takes a picture again, under the supposition that the person has moved into a new place.

This obsession with ordering is filling more and more of our intellectual and emotional spaces. The construction of Wikipedia has more ordering behind it than most users realize. It's not just a very long series of entries but rather those articles must be organized and divvied up and that leads to debates about the proper method of ordering. For instance some Wikipedia editors and fans are "Mergists," who believe that shorter articles should generally be merged into longer ones. In fact the very discussion of Mergism has now been merged into the Wikipedia entry on Deletionism and Inclusionism, quite possibly to the extreme nerdy delight of the person who did the merging.

The Inclusionists believe that information should be added liberally to Wikipedia. The Deletionists are upset about articles that are too trivial to belong. The Inclusionists say "Wikipedia is not paper"; the Deletionists say "Wikipedia is not Google" or they note that Wikipedia is not a dumping ground for facts. If you want to catch a glimpse of some occasional personal viciousness, just read the online Wikipedia debates about whether a marginal person's Wikipedia entry should be deleted. Among the goals of the Mergists is to "outpace rampant Inclusionism and Deletionism."

The debate does not stop there. There is a difference between Deletionism and the apparently similar (but not) philosophy of Exclusionism. There is also Eventualism, Incrementalism, Immediatism, and at least two different spectrums for debate, namely Mergism-Separatism and Exopedianism-Metapedianism. And if that is not enough ordered structure for you there is the Association of Wikipedians Who Dislike Making Broad Judgments About the Worthiness of a General Category of Article, and Who Are in Favor of the Deletion of Some Particularly Bad Articles, but That Doesn't Mean They Are Deletionists. Let's just say Wikipedia has some people thinking about some workable methods for ordering it.

The point is not that we all need to become Buddhists, as that is a personal theological decision. But Buddhism does identify some very real costs and biases of mental ordering. If we engage in too much mental ordering—fun though it may be—we can lose sight of "the whole" and we can lose sight of the path toward greater harmony within ourselves. And yes, mental ordering can lead us to frustration, in part because the order is never completed. Or if the order were completed we might feel unfulfilled or disappointed, just as when we finally collect every baseball card for a given year of play.

The Buddhist critique, however, does not provide a larger-scale refutation of mental ordering. Mental ordering is important in ways that are not emphasized adequately in Buddhist philosophy, namely:

- Mental ordering is very often a joy.
- There is a multiplicity of paths toward freedom, and mental ordering can be one of them; it is one way of realizing individual autonomy.
- We use mental ordering to establish intense, emotional connections with other people, such as when we go on Facebook and order our friends, photos, and experiences.
- The brain is not infinitely plastic, so many people will experience above-average levels of specialized mental ordering as part of their destinies; we should accept this tendency and build on its strengths rather than always working to overcome it or eliminate it.
- Even Buddhist meditation can be ordered. There are websites where you can record, track, and even upload your meditation experiences.

In other words, mental ordering can be fun and productive, and it isn't going away.

Buddhism cannot fully regulate mental ordering any more than it can restructure the sensual side of human life. Consider the analogy of Tantric Buddhism. The Tantric philosophy also attempts to reshape the human mind. When you hear the word "Tantric" or "Tantra" you may think of sex books, but that is usually a modern corruption of a much older and more serious set of religious ideas, some but not all of which concerned sex. In any case Tantric Buddhism does address the sensual pleasures of human beings. Just as mental ordering can obstruct inner harmony and mindfulness, so can sensual pleasure.

The Tantric ideal is to allow people to reconceive their visceral and sensual pleasures in a refined way and so—counterintuitively, to many—to use sensual pleasure as another path to Buddhist harmony and nirvana.

If Tantric philosophy is helping us broaden our sense of the erotic and the sensual, it is a wonderful supplement to the more mainstream understanding of what sex is all about. But if Tantric philosophy is suppressing basic human nature and trying to impose uniformity on our appreciation of the sensual, it will fail. That qualification of Tantrism makes good intuitive sense to most people; I'm saying that insofar as Buddhism tries to suppress mental ordering it will be no more successful and no more liberating.

Unlike Buddhism, New Age religions do not have much intellectual respectability but often they are getting at some core Buddhist ideas (and ideas from other Eastern religions). If you look at recent bestsellers like *The Secret,* the numerous works of Deepak Chopra, or *The Celestine Prophecy,* among others, you'll find they are largely echoing themes from Eastern religions. Most of all these works stress the quest for positive thinking and the simplification of our lives.

It's easy to rail against the oversimplifications of these books but I view their ascendancy as an implicit recognition of just how powerful mental ordering has become. You don't need books like *The Celestine Prophecy* to give you a balanced or sophisticated perspective on the human condition. Instead you use the book to push back against what you are experiencing in your life, namely the daily pressures and the chaos and the intense mental ordering. You turn the book, or the parts of it you've read, into a bit of protest on the side of serenity and calm. ("Serenity now!" was the saying barked out by the characters in *Seinfeld*.) It's your substitute for running off and becoming a Buddhist monk, which you don't really want to do anyway.

One of the most alluring forms of excess is *collecting,* in particular collecting to the point where the completion of the collection becomes an obsession. You can think of collecting as a form of mental ordering, often aided by the intermediation of commodities. Sometimes the collecting focuses on physical objects but other times it is a form of mental collecting through the assemblage of lists and ordered memories; the mental collecting of unusual words is another habit. Ultimately all collecting is the collecting of information. Of course it's not just autistics who collect enthusiastically, so the following remarks apply quite generally.

Collecting is a double-edged sword. Collecting is in part about who you are and what you value; people collect not only to "get the stuff" but also to fill out the pieces of their personal narratives. Collecting can be a means of encountering the world, broadening one's horizons, and developing fun and meaningful quests. It gives emotional resonance to what you've done and experienced. Most of all the collected stuff is fun or intense in an interesting way and of course it creates framing effects that enhance your broader life. An art collection can make your home beautiful or a music collection can bring compelling sounds into your life. That said, sometimes a collection can be stifling. Too often collecting focuses on completion of a particular ordered set and that can make collecting a potential source of frustration. Economists refer to "the problem of complements." If you need just one item to fill out your set, and you care about having a complete set, you might pay a great deal to get that final item and that can make collecting very expensive and very troublesome.

Unfortunately, when it comes to collecting the lines are not so easy to draw. We might flatter ourselves by thinking we are happy collectors, but the psychological literature on collecting suggests that happy collecting is not always the case. We all collect something but collecting is a limited, repetitive process. Freud identified collecting with an anal-compulsive fastidiousness. I don't think his terminology exactly reflects the reality but he intuitively sensed the frustrating element behind collecting. Collecting often turns into an obsession:

> Frank Keillor, a 54-year-old watch and fountain pen collector who lives in Moss Beach, would be disinclined to cast his potterings in philosophical terms. Poised over a ground-floor workbench in his oceanside home and surrounded by the minute parts and tools of the watchmaker's trade, he says cheerfully, "I'm a nerd. I love to take things apart and see how they work."
>
> Keillor owns about 200 watches and several dozen prized fountain pens. He can rattle off the provenance and mechanical subtleties of his 1970s "working-class" watches and extol the virtues of flexible iridium pen tips, piston ink fillers, and cellulose barrels. "I know, I know," he says. "I see people's eyes glaze over when I get started."
>
> Why do they do it?
>
> Like many collectors, Keillor initially comes up blank when asked why he got started and why watches and pens.

It is possible that Keillor has fallen into what I call a collecting trap. It is also possible that he has a deep understanding of the aesthetic virtues of watches and pens. Or both.

It's not obvious what "the normal amount of collecting" is supposed to be. M. Fauron, onetime president of a cigar band collectors' association, said that a person who does not collect something is "nothing but a moron, a pathetic human wreck." It is easy to laugh at that statement as a kind of joke or overstatement, but is it? A person who does not in some way order his mental and emotional existence perhaps has not much of an existence at all.

Nonetheless it is easy enough to spot the excesses. There's a club of people who have visited one hundred countries or more (the Travelers' Century Club) and many people aspire to join. I am skeptical and I think of these people as "country collectors" who probably don't understand "real travel" at all. Maybe I'm the one who is irrational but I see real travel as requiring a few favorite places and "collecting" emotional memories and artifacts of those places to an intense degree. That's consistent with visiting lots of countries overall, and alternating your favorite places against new places, but you can't get to one hundred countries that way unless you are a sailor or an airplane pilot, and maybe not even then. Besides, should it matter where the line is drawn between one country and another? If I've visited the former East and West Germany, as I did in 1985, does that count as one country or still two? What if you stepped foot in Kiev before Ukraine was independent? Have you been to "Ukraine" or not? Why should you count the number of countries at all?

Charles Veley was labeled by *The New York Times* as the world's most traveled man. He is only forty-three years old but after making a good deal of money from a software company he set out to see the world. By the age of thirty-seven he became the world's youngest man to have visited all 317 countries (perhaps not surprisingly, not everyone accepts that as the correct number of countries). Veley was frustrated when Guinness World Records ruled that his claims were not verifiable. So he set up his own website—mosttraveledpeople. com—to record his feats and document that he is in fact the world's best-traveled man. At the center of the website is a list of the world's ten most traveled people (at least by Veley's standards) and of course he is a clear number one. The standards are explicit: "In the case of islands where landing is prohibited by law due to wildlife concerns or other natural heritage status, it is acceptable to touch a portion of the island above the waterline (whether while swimming or from a boat) in lieu of landing." Veley, by the way, has a wife and three small children back home in San Francisco, so he doesn't stay very long in any single travel locale. "I travel so much because I can," Veley says.

One acquaintance (self-described Asperger's) once told me: "Every now and then I notice myself starting to collect something. I pull myself together and then I stop." But why stop? Isn't the collecting fun? Maybe so, but still we fear an overinvolvement in mental ordering. An overfixation on programs of completion can paint you into some inflexible corners. The take-home message here is that we need the freedom to rebel against stories of completion and wander in new directions.

OK, so we can think of Buddhism as a potential offset to some of the problems with mental ordering. What is the corresponding offset to the very different problems of people who do not engage in *enough* mental ordering? I have at least one answer, namely *education*. But like Buddhism, in light of a sometimes recalcitrant human nature it doesn't always work.

As an entry into this topic, let's look at the reasons why people become educated.

Economists cite three central motivations behind education. First, we go to school to learn something. Second, we go to school to demonstrate our smarts and perseverance, or in other words to show that we can "jump through hoops." Economists call this the "signaling model of education." Third, we go to school because it is (sometimes) fun. Of course the relative weight of these three motivations will depend upon the level of education, the school in question, and also on the personality of the individual in question.

I have one other explanation, not inconsistent with the traditional list, but with a slightly different emphasis. I view education as a means of acculturation into a particular mind-set.

There is plenty of evidence on acculturation and you can see it most clearly by examining the lives of migrants. If you move from Vietnam to America at age seven, you very likely grow up, culturally speaking, as an American. You will think like an American, have an American accent, and have a largely American view of the world. You'll still probably have a partly Vietnamese sense of obligations to family, but in cultural terms you probably will have no trouble "fitting in." If you move from Vietnam at age thirteen, you still adopt many American cultural mores although it's not like coming over as a seven-year-old. If you switch cultures at age eighteen, it is harder to say. If you move from Vietnam to Portland at age twenty-five, you probably stay fairly Vietnamese although you will pick up many American habits. Of course the more time you spend with Americans the more American you will become. If you move from Mexico at age four and grow up in a community of other Mexican migrants, you may adopt the attitudes of that peer group.

The bottom line is this: For most people a large part of your cultural identity and worldview is shaped by what you are doing, and by the identity of your peers, between the critical ages of something like eight and twenty years old.

Those comparisons help us understand our educational system. Education is in part a self-commitment to being a more productive kind of person. Education is about *self*-acculturation. Education gives you a peer group, a self-image, and also some skills. Getting an education is like becoming a Marine. Men (and women) need to be *made* into Marines because they are not usually born that way. By choosing many years of education, you are telling yourself that you stand on one side of a social divide rather than the other. The education itself drums that truth into you and the internalization of that attitude is above and beyond anything specific you learned at school.

Similarly, if you become a Mormon or an evangelical Protestant in Central America, your lifetime earnings prospects go up, at least on average. It is not that Mormons have necessarily learned so much more, but rather they have acquired a different sense of self. They have a more positive self-image about their destiny in life, about their commercial ambitions, and they choose different peers. They also choose not to drink.

No one ever tells you exactly how schooling is supposed to work, but I have a hypothesis. Few if any people would put it this way, but I view school as teaching people to be just a bit more autistic in their cognitive skills. Indeed so much of school is about encouraging focus, cognitive specialization, and mental ordering. Students are taught how to concentrate, how to finish the task at hand, how to avoid distraction, and why education isn't just about socializing. At least that's what we as educators try to teach our students.

There is a lot of evidence that contemporary Americans, however powerful some of their abilities and ambitions, are not always so good at focusing. Try this question:

Amanda wants to paint each face of a cube a different color. How many colors will she need?

(A) Three   **(B)** Four   **(C)** Six   **(D)** Eight

Sadly 20 percent of a sample of eighth graders did not know that the correct answer is (C), namely that a cube has six sides.

Now why did so many students get this wrong? My guess is that they can count to six and my guess is that they know what an ice cube is and thus they know what a cube is. Most likely, they simply didn't focus on the question in the right way to convert these pieces of knowledge into a correct answer.

The tougher the problem, the more focus is needed. Another question postulated a company with ninety employees and then noted that the number of employees rose by 10 percent. How many employees did the company then have? Only 38 percent of sampled eighth graders got the correct answer of ninety-nine and of course some of them were guessing, so the percentage who really understood the problem was lower yet. You can attribute some of the mistakes to bad arithmetic but again I think focus was a major problem.

Isn't the proverbial educational image that of a teacher coming over to the sixth-grade student and telling him or her, "Stop your daydreaming!" In the old days this might have been accompanied by a rap on the knuckles. Well, there was a recent study from the University of San Diego based on brain scans. One conclusion was that autistic people engage in "internally directed resting thoughts" to a lesser degree than do non-autistics. While further associations are speculative, the notion of daydreaming plausibly belongs to this category, or in other words maybe autistics daydream less than do non-autistics. The researchers believe that autistics may instead prefer to focus on a smaller number of preferred items of attention. In the context of the scientific literature this is called a cognitive disability of autism but of course it is what every teacher is trying (and usually failing) to achieve in the classroom.

According to the Department of Education, in the year 2001–2002 Americans spent over $731 billion on formal education at all levels. That's a lot of money. I've never seen a good breakdown of how much of that money went to real learning, how much went to pleasure (nice college dorms, mowing the campus lawn, playtime in kindergarten, and so on), and how much went to the signaling function of education, such as enforcing standards and making sure that admitted students have high test scores. But just as a stab in the dark, let's say that one tenth of that money went to teaching students how to focus and engage in structured mental ordering. That's over $70 billion we would spend each year to make our kids—dare I say it—in behavioral terms more like autistics. Or so we hope, even though many people would recoil at that terminology.

Without at least a decent education, non-autistics do much less well in life and they have only a small chance at worldly success. If you go to parts of the world where people do not get formal educations, you will find that reading, writing, and even basic counting skills are extremely limited. Most of these people would have serious difficulties adapting to a middle-class American lifestyle and its concomitant demands. Analogously, most autistics do not get good educations suited to their special needs and that is one (but by no means the only) reason for many of their difficulties in life. Autistics are not competing on the proverbial "level playing field," as virtually all educational institutions are designed for the non-autistic. Many autistics experience schools as somewhere along the spectrum between "useless" and "torture."

You'll notice that many nerds dislike school even though they love learning. Furthermore many "economist nerds" embrace the signaling model of education, as that notion was explained above, and they hold such a model as their dominant account of what education is. One core assumption of the signaling model is that, insofar as education is signaling, you don't learn much of value. Nonetheless you still have to go to school, if only to prove you have "the right stuff." By sitting through college, and perhaps a doctoral degree or MBA, you prove to potential employers (and mates) that you are a smart and diligent person. After all, your education was lots of hard work and finishing really does show something about your skill and perseverance even if you weren't always in the midst of valuable learning.

I think the signaling model explains a good deal of the education sector but many of the economist nerds overrate the importance of signaling. They also underrate the importance of education in acculturating people and thus making them more productive. I think the economist nerds, and believe me I know these people, make this mistake because of their introspection and because of their own lives. If you are an economist nerd, your sense of self and your commitment to the importance of focus and intellect is usually formed quite early. As a result, so much of school seems like a waste of time. It seems like a series of ridiculous jumps through hoops, to return to that analogy. But still education instills good values in most people, especially the value of focus and some of the abilities required for mental ordering.

It is clear that many people on the autism spectrum will have less need for the kinds of educational conditioning that are prevalent today. They may desire the learning but they don't need the same kind of acculturation into the notion of focus. If it's something an autistic person wishes to study, he or she already will be studying it and studying it past the level and dedication of a top honors student.

But there's a funny thing about how our schools try to teach kids to be "more autistic" in the sense of achieving this focused specialization. They don't do a very good job at it. In essence schools are using social means to teach kids to be more like the autistic. It's no wonder that such a paradoxical undertaking doesn't always work.

That may sound a little weird—"schools are using social means to teach kids to be more like the autistic"—so let me explain.

When I think about my personal role in education, as an instructor, I sometimes wonder: Why do my students need *me*? Why can't they listen to someone else? They don't have to fly to Harvard or MIT, they just need a DVD player and an internet connection. Maybe an iPhone would do.

Let's say for instance that Greg Mankiw and recent Nobel laureate

Paul Krugman are two of the sharper economic minds of the last few decades. It's not hard to record their lectures on DVD and sell them. I'm just not the most eloquent economist out there. Since many professors are giving those lectures anyway, it can't cost so much extra to record them and perhaps to reproduce their lecture notes as well. Note that both Mankiw and Krugman have written very successful principles-of-economics textbooks, so clearly they are willing to put time into popular education if the remuneration is there and perhaps even for free (both have had doctoral students, which is in essence an unpaid form of volunteer work).

The Teaching Company makes high-quality tapes of lectures by outstanding professors. It's a fine company and they offer some excellent products, but they're not a competitive threat to higher education in this country. If anything, I suspect the company boosts the hold of higher education by making more people aspire to greater knowledge, thereby increasing the long-run demand for in-person instruction. It is interesting that the demand for top colleges, and the price of college tuition, has taken off at exactly the same time as the internet revolution. I'm not suggesting that the spread of the internet caused this boom in quality higher education, but it does indicate the internet will not displace such education.

And if taping lectures seems too hard, or perhaps the rights are difficult to negotiate, how about just sitting at home and reading the textbook? (Heaven forbid.) Most people in college can read faster than they can listen to someone else speak.

You might think that a conspiracy of colleges and universities is stopping DVD-based or web-based instruction from spreading, but I find that hard to believe. There aren't many restrictions on what can be put on YouTube or what can be marketed on disc. The main problem is that if you received such an education, the so-called real world—most of all employers—wouldn't much respect it. Just try putting on your vita "Watched YouTube lectures for four years" and see how far you get. Listing the videos wouldn't much help you, no matter how good the list might look on paper. The real world is the constraint, not some monopolistic cabal in the upper reaches of higher education.

The reality is that most education requires the physical presence of other human beings. The flesh-and-blood instructor motivates students better and the presence of other students in the classroom makes the experience more vivid and memorable. Our proximity to both the leader (the professor) and the peers (the fellow students) means that we end up more interested, more focused, and more able to succeed in later life. As human beings most of us (but not all of us) are biologically programmed to respond positively to face time with others.

I call it *education as theater.* And it is not a one-man or one-woman show. Education as theater may be highly inefficient compared to some ideal of how we might absorb knowledge, but for most people it seems like the best we can do.

I've tried lecturing to an empty hall for the purposes of the recording camera. It's very hard to summon up the same enthusiasm and to make the stories memorable or funny without an admiring crowd. The point isn't that getting good tapes is impossible (put a real crowd in and tape the lecture), but rather that interpersonal connection is so often what motivates. If that is how the already-educated professor responds to the empty room, the indifferent reactions of a student to an empty room will be an even bigger problem.

We love the internet but when we go online we pursue our very personal agendas and interests and we spend most of our time connecting with other people. It's the very fun of that process that makes it so hard to master the derivation of income elasticity in Greg Mankiw's *Principles of Economics* text. There's always something better to do. Even when our friends are all away or at work, isn't the distraction of the internet ever-present? Not that many people go web cruising to spend their time on dry lesson plans. So schools use face-to-face education to connect the idea of income elasticity with a human personality and a human presentation.

For the most part, television and the movies have replaced live theater in the United States and other wealthy countries. In that context it seems we don't all need the live, personalized performances. So how does that differ from higher education? Well, TV can replace live theater because when the TV show is over, no one is expected to go out and do some hard work as a result of what the actors said. We remain passive spectators and more often than not we watch yet another show. But when we need to be motivated and inspired, it's person-to-person contact that does the trick for most of us. Preachers, missionaries, and professional fund-raisers all will tell you the same thing. Similarly, not all business meetings can be displaced by videoconferencing, again because personal contact is so often needed.

The music industry understands this point well. If you see a rock and roll band live in concert, you are much more likely to become a dedicated fan. That's one of the main reasons why musical acts tour, namely to develop rapport with audiences, collect together peer groups, and stimulate fandom. All that contact encourages purchases of the recorded music. This importance of personal contact is maybe the only way in which being a professor is like being a rock star.

Once you start to think about the problem in these terms, you start asking further questions about just how effective education is. There are plenty of studies that measure the economic "rate of return" on education and these studies come up with fairly high numbers. In other words, if you graduate from college, or with a postgraduate degree, you will earn more. But what are these studies comparing education to? It's now well-known in the medical literature that a medicine needs to be compared to a placebo, rather than to simply doing nothing. Placebo effects can be very powerful and many supposedly effective medicines do not in fact outperform the placebo. The sorry truth is that no one has compared modern education to a placebo. What if we just gave people lots of face-to-face contact and *told* them they were being educated?

I'm not sure I want to know the answer to that question. Maybe that's what current methods of education *already consist of.*

So again, most of us need the influence of the leader, the crowd, and the face time to enforce focus on the academic material. Or to go back to my original contention, education is using social influences to encourage autistic cognitive skills.

Of course non-autistics experience so much educational failure, in part, because many people can increase their focus only so much. That's yet another bias and it is a bias that so many of us suffer under. The lesson is this: No matter what your neurology, be careful whom you criticize. It may just be someone you should be trying to emulate.

6

THE NEW ECONOMY OF STORIES

There has been a fundamental shift in the balance of power between consumers and salesmen over the last generation and it points in the direction of consumers. The quantity and quality of "interior" pleasures is higher than ever before, so many people shift more toward these very cheap entertainments.

Because of this rise of interiority, we're saving money on our learning and entertainment and we're also telling ourselves more stories. Stories are a big part of how we think, so an account of education, or of self-education, should ask the tough questions. If you are looking to create your own economy, what role should stories play in that process? Should you embrace your tendency to use the narrative mode or should you be suspicious of it?

One good approach to understanding the costs and benefits of story-based reasoning is to start with . . . a story.

In 1984 Thomas C. Schelling published a fascinating yet neglected article called "The Mind as a Consuming Organ." Schelling is a former Harvard professor and a Nobel laureate in economics. Schelling won the Nobel Prize for his analysis of strategic behavior and game theory, especially as he applied those ideas to military conflict and nuclear deterrence, and he finds most of his readers in those areas. "The Mind as a Consuming Organ" was never published in a professional refereed journal and if anything it has attracted more attention from political scientists. Nonetheless it's Schelling at his best.

Schelling is a curious character, as anyone who knows him will attest. (I am honored to report he was my doctoral adviser.) Upon first meeting he doesn't seem like a world-class intellect. He has the down-to-earth demeanor of a man who has been selling Hush Puppy shoes in the local mall for the last thirty years. He has short hair, a slight build, and a welcoming smile. When he encounters an idea he usually responds in a roundabout manner. You might hear a story about how he tried to quit smoking, what his grandmother used to tell him, or why terrorists won't want to use any nuclear weapons they happen to acquire. Typically, at first you think that Schelling didn't listen to what you said because his story seems so off base; a minute later you realize that maybe he has a point, albeit a wrong one; five minutes later you understand he was well ahead of you the entire time.

The interesting thing is, Schelling usually presents his ideas in terms of stories. This is unusual in a profession obsessed with mathematics and formal modeling. No matter what you say to him, Tom will start thinking about which kind of story might be relevant for formulating an insightful response. And once he starts narrating, he gets a dreamy look in his eye and no one wants to interrupt. The interjections and qualifications to the story are often as good as the main narrative itself.

The essay "The Mind as a Consuming Organ," as usual, draws

upon Schelling's personal musings. How many other economists start their essays with a sentence like "Lassie died one night"? Here's the whole opening:

> Lassie died one night. Millions of viewers, not all of them children, grieved. At least, they shed tears. Except for the youngest, the mourners knew that Lassie didn't really exist. Whatever that means. Perhaps with their left hemispheres they could articulate that they had been watching a trained dog and that *that* dog was still alive, healthy, and rich; meanwhile in their right hemispheres, or some such place (if these phenomena have a place), the real Lassie had died.
>
> Did they enjoy the episode?

Schelling emphasizes that we "consume" stories through memories, anticipations, fantasies, and daydreams. Concrete goods and services, such as Lassie programs, help impose order and discipline on our fantasies and give us stronger and more coherent mental lives.

Of course consuming stories is not just about watching television, even though the average American does that for several hours in a typical day. If the tube bores us, we play computer games, read novels, reimagine central events in our lives, spin fantasies, or listen to the narratives of our friends. A successful blog is often about the Bildungsroman, or life development, of its author. Even watching the news, or following a presidential campaign, is in large part driven by our nearly insatiable demand for stories, even if it is stories about politicians. Consuming stories is not just a sideshow to the broader economic problem but rather it is one of the central human passions and one of the central sources of our well-being, including our satisfaction as consumers.

You're not just buying a sneaker, you're buying an image of athleticism and an associated story about yourself. It's not just an indie pop song, it is your sense of identity as the listener and owner of the music. If you give to Oxfam, yes you want to help people, but you also are constructing a narrative about your place in the broader world and the responsibilities you have chosen to assume.

The Portuguese author Fernando Pessoa wrote: "The buyers of useless things are wiser than is commonly supposed—they buy little dreams." That is a big part of what markets are about. Whether you are buying cosmetics, a lottery ticket, or an oil painting, you are constructing, defining, and memorializing your dreams into vivid and physically real forms. Gabriel García Márquez, in his *Living to Tell the Tale* (*Vivir Para Contarla* so "Living in Order to Tell It" is arguably a better or at least a more literal translation), understood the power of stories. His opening quotation notes: "Life is not what one lived, but what one remembers and how one remembers it in order to recount it."

It's not just Márquez; there is a long-standing "underground" Spanish- and Portuguese-language tradition stressing the story-bound nature of our lives, derived most of all from Cervantes's *Don Quixote*. The Don starts the novel living in a dream of his own making. As the narrative progresses in book 2, the Don takes the numerous stories written about him and Sancho Panza to be his major touchstone for reality and he lives in reference to those stories. It's the contrast between the published works on the Don's adventures and how he interprets those works in his mind that creates the framework of meaning for the Don's quests. I think of *Don Quixote* as providing some of the earliest glimpses into how to live a life by assembling small cultural bits and in the process spinning a story about yourself (and your loved ones) from those bits. In this sense *Don Quixote* is the first truly modern or perhaps even contemporary novel. The Don is assembling bits about himself by drawing upon the commercial culture of his time, namely the enormous secondary literature of tracts, pamphlets, and books based on his (fictional) exploits with Sancho Panza.

It may sound like I'm talking only about literature but I'm also talking about economics. I think of people as creating their own economies inside their heads.

When it comes to understanding the social world, the individual human mind really does matter. Traditional economics is reasonably good at predicting how people behave in a variety of well-defined environments, especially when people understand the nature of the constraints they are facing. If the price of coffee goes up, people will go to Starbucks less often. If income goes up, people will seek out safer rather than riskier jobs; you will find poor Honduran immigrants rather than wealthy heiresses working on dangerous fishing boats. To understand these matters we can turn to traditional economics and do without broader contextual knowledge about human psychology.

But those are not the most fundamental questions about our world. Traditional economics has a tougher time with "What do people believe?" and "How do people order their internal realities?" and "How does that order shape our emotions?" Yet without a grasp on those issues, economics will fail repeatedly, most of all when we are trying to understand large-scale social phenomena. For instance economics has failed at predicting or even understanding stock market crashes and changes in social fads, and at addressing straightforward questions like why you can't always just pay people to follow your managerial orders. (Partial answer: If people *believe* you are trying to control them with the money, rather than reward them, they will rebel rather than cooperate in response to the offered payment.)

In other words, human perceptions are all-important for understanding how incentives translate into outcomes. Unless you know how people *think* the world works, you can't predict their behavior very well. And sometimes human perceptions are at odds with reality. Remember the run-up toward the second Iraq War when Saddam Hussein stonewalled and refused to give in to then-President Bush? It turned out that, according to later evidence, Hussein never thought that Bush would actually send U.S. troops through to Baghdad. What Bush thought was deterrence was viewed as an empty bluff. Saddam, at the same time, thought it very important that the Iranians *believe* he had weapons of mass destruction. And so he pretended he did and of course he fooled many other people as well. A traditional economist might find Hussein's behavior puzzling, or he might describe it as "irrational." After all, Saddam Hussein ended up losing a country, his freedom, his sense of honor, and then his life. But a focus on the importance of belief suggests that the evil and tragic saga of Saddam Hussein is in fact a very human story based on some common imperfections.

One of the most fundamental truths about the social world is that objective reality does not determine what people believe. Or in the language of economics, expectations are not generally rational.

People misperceive reality or people self-deceive to construct a more pleasant reality within their own minds. Or sometimes we prefer the tragic, such as when we tune in to watch Lassie die. Maybe some people are just plain flat-out unable to figure out how things work. Most significantly, we interpret real-world evidence through our stories and through the internal ordering imposed by our minds.

Here's a simple schema of how economics fits into this broader view of social science:

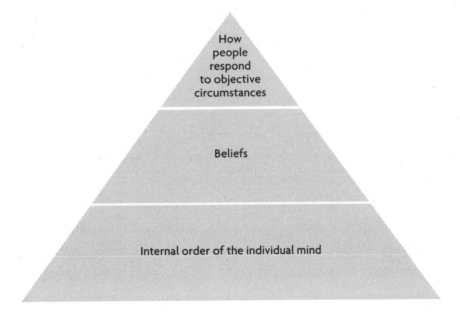

Traditional economics focuses on the top of the pyramid, namely how people respond to objective changes, such as changes in incentives. (Perhaps the other social sciences don't focus *enough* on incentives, but that is another story.) But it's not enough to think in terms of incentives because all incentives are set and interpreted in a particular context, and that brings in psychology. The deeper foundational questions—namely the nature of the individual mind—are at the base of the pyramid and indeed at the base of all the social sciences. So you can think of this book as a rebellion against traditional economics or as a micro-foundation for a better economics or as neuroeconomics; alternatively, I view it as a return home to the original foundations of economics.

It may come as a surprise that the origin of the study of economics was substantially psychology, perception, and mental ordering. As I've already discussed, Adam Smith, the father of modern economics, wrote not just *The Wealth of Nations* but also a book on human psychology, namely *The Theory of Moral Sentiments*. Smith's life's work was to mix economic reasoning with Stoic moral philosophy (Seneca, Epictetus, and Marcus Aurelius, plus their French Renaissance successor Montaigne) and applied psychology, most of which he generated from his own reasoning. The Stoics were themselves obsessed with the proper internal order of the mind and in particular how to manage pain, how to deal with what you can never have, and how to lower your expectations so that life seems like a pleasure rather than a burden. Whereas the Stoics sought to understand the psychology of the Roman Empire, exile, and the slave whip, and Smith studied the pin factory, I am looking at Facebook, Google, and the iPod.

The later and more general movement of "behavioral economics" has brought psychology very directly into economics. In addition to all the formal research, behavioral economics is represented by such popular books as Dan Ariely's *Predictably Irrational,* Richard Thaler and Cass Sunstein's *Nudge,* and Ori and Rom Brafman's *Sway.* In the most general terms, behavioral economics suggests that human decision-making is often far from rational. For instance maybe we overestimate our prospects of success when we start a new business or maybe we are very bad at evaluating risks with very small probabilities. In the behavioral view we are ruled by emotions and often we use dysfunctional decision-making procedures and rules. However reasonable we may claim to be, so often reason just doesn't stick. Behavioral economics has made economics more realistic and arguably it is the single most influential trend in the economics profession today.

I'm all for behavioral economics and if you wish, you can think of this book as a study in behavioral economics. Nonetheless I am going beyond standard behavioral approaches in at least four ways. First, I emphasize neurodiversity—in this case the autism spectrum—as an important feature of human diversity. This investigation is a kind of neuroeconomics but not as that word usually is employed. Most of current neuroeconomics assumes that people are the same and scans their brains while they make economic decisions in the lab; the goal is to uncover which part of the brain made the decision and thus to understand whether the decision was ruled by fear, the prospect of reward, and so on. In contrast, I start with the natural neurological differences between human beings and see how those differences shape real-world outcomes.

Second, I focus on contemporary culture and the web, two topics that behavioral economists and neuroeconomists have neglected. Third, the analysis is dynamic. Most behavioral studies look at human psychology at a single point in time, such as how psychology might affect the pricing of mutual funds or the placement of the milk in a supermarket (it's almost always in the back, to spur impulse purchases of candy and soda as you walk to get your dairy). In contrast, I am asking how the evolution of culture and technology will make a *difference* for modern life and how it will alter the relative importance of our cognitive strengths and weaknesses.

Finally, I emphasize the notion of stories. Although analyzing stories is prominent in what is called "narrative psychology," the notion of stories has yet to have much impact on behavioral economics, even though most people love to think in terms of stories. Most people are programmed to think in terms of stories and they have an especially good memory for stories. "The economics of stories" is one of the next frontiers in social science but most economists are still behind the curve, with the exception of course of Thomas Schelling.

Once you consider the power of stories, the traditional economist's notion of scarcity becomes inverted. Traditional economics is usually about acquiring things and thus overcoming scarcity, but a lot of human behavior is about *creating* artificial scarcity and then choosing a quest. Quests, which I define as stories of overcoming scarcity, require at least two kinds of scarcity. First, if you want to go on a meaningful quest, you must be lacking in something. Second, the protagonist cannot focus on everything and thus must choose and discard priorities to define a preferred quest.

Stories and quests are very old and time-honored methods of mental ordering. But the ordering isn't just about arranging a set of given units or concerns, as you might file a collection of baseball cards. Discarding and whittling down are fundamental features of this ordering process, which has something in common with cleaning out an old bureau. Stories aren't just about creating context and building. Stories also require us to take away or eliminate material to make the resulting pieces cohere, stick in our minds, and constitute a plot based on a struggle to achieve something. In essence the new cultural economics is about how corporate marketing and individual self-assembly combine to create stories of meaning based on quests, scarcity, and uncertainty.

The Lord of the Rings works so well as a popular story precisely because the major characters do not have magical powers; that said, the idea of magic shapes their quest and the excitement of magic continually titillates the imagination of Tolkien's readers. Frodo and his band spend most of the story tracking down a very powerful ring. Once the ring's fate is determined the story is essentially over and it is time to sum up the fate of each character and close the book.

Most good fantasy stories offer elaborate explanations of what kinds of angelic transformations are possible, what you must do to hunt down a unicorn, and what limits are placed on magic powers. Readers will forgive just about any kind of unrealism, as long as the rules are consistently enforced.

"Why can't the long-separated prince and princess just come together and marry?" a naïve child might ask, but having seen the movie *The Princess Bride* you know better. Kidnappings, masked men, babies switched at birth, dragons guarding borders, and warring kingdoms are common plot devices, all designed to make sure that not everything comes too easily. Harlequin novels offer up their own constraints, most notably social prejudices and forbidding fathers, common themes in Bollywood as well. If the stories bore quickly, it is because there are only so many ways of summoning up admiration from afar and then maintaining the tension. And if the romantic fantasy has cyber communication between the two protagonists, such as in the Tom Hanks/Meg Ryan movie *You've Got Mail*, the two parties can't know each other's real-world identities until the end of the movie approaches. Of course stories of constraint are getting harder to write in this modern, information-rich age of communication and this is one reason why dramatists set so many of their tales in the past.

Samantha, the protagonist of the old television series *Bewitched*, faces the same problem that Harry Potter does. The drama works only if there are limits to her magic. In part the show solves this problem by having Samantha vow to live among mortals and eschew her magic (n.b.: she doesn't always keep the agreement, so the viewer faces some probability of titillation). And in part the show works because Samantha is hard at work on one of the most difficult problems of all: creating and sustaining a happy marriage, in this case with the mortal man Darrin, her husband.

More people are transfixed by Dante's *Inferno* than by Dante's *Paradiso*. It's not that we all are Satan worshippers or secretly aspire to be sent to the tortures of hell. It's simpler, namely that paradise doesn't usually make for good fiction. If you look closely at the structure of Dante's poem, he keeps the tale of paradise interesting only by a series of literary tricks, such as postponing entry into paradise, recapitulating the journey to date, and recapping the narrator's inner psychological tensions. In other words, it's not really a tale of paradise at all because paradise has no need of epic poetry. You know the end of the poem is approaching when Dante writes: "And so my pen skips and I do not write it, for our imagination is too crude, as is our speech, to paint the subtler colors of the fields of bliss."

I'm suggesting that these difficulties in constructing fictional narratives reflect broader difficulties in how we bring meaning into our lives and how we make our personal stories cohere. In a mental universe with no story-based hierarchical principles, you're a hungry and ravenous being trying to own or consume as many commodities or bits of information as possible. In a story-based view, in contrast, very often you already have more bits than you know what to do with. We whittle away at the thicket of information and organize some bits in the form of narratives, even if that means we end up with fewer bits overall.

In this vision of how we create mental value, the economic problem is again what to toss away—and how to order what is left—and not just what to acquire. An "economics of stories" gives the notion of mental ordering a central importance.

Of course the richer we become, the more likely our predicament is one of finding the proper ordering rather than just acquiring more. We have access to lots more "stuff" than ever before, if only through the internet, but our available time does not rise in proportion. So again we organize goods, services, and events into favored stories and jettison that which does not fit.

Story-based forms of mental ordering are a bit different from observed tendencies for many autistics. There is some evidence that autistics are less likely than non-autistics to think in terms of stories and also less likely to have highly vivid story-based dreams. This is hardly a settled area in science but autistics seem to impose different kinds of mental order on information and those orders seem to have a more specialized, more intense, and less narrative focus. It is common for autistics to strongly prefer reading nonfiction to reading fiction. There is also evidence that autistics have a weaker sense of episodic memory, even when their memory skills are strong overall. The memories of autistics are thus less likely to end up stored as emotionally misleading or biasing stories and more likely to be stored as a series of facts. Arguably autistics are less likely to be the ones thirsting for personal revenge, although I have not seen this particular claim studied formally.

In any case, for most people a successful story, like a successful celebrity, must be socially salient. A salient story, quite simply, is one that is memorable, emotionally resonant, and can be explained easily to most other people.

This point about salience returns us to Thomas Schelling and one of his other major contributions to social science. It was Schelling who developed the idea of "focal points." A focal point refers to something we all can coordinate around without having to talk about it or plan it in advance. You might say if your boss invites you to present at a meeting of the company's board of directors, it is focal that you wear a tie, even if no one tells you to. At Google headquarters casual dress usually is expected and thus they have a different focal point. Most generally a focal point is a commonly understood social expectation.

The concept of a focal point makes me recall the words of Jim Sinclair, an autistic who writes on the web. He informs us: "DON'T TAKE ANYTHING FOR GRANTED. Don't assume you can interpret the [autistic] person's behavior by comparing it with your own or other people's behavior . . . Don't assume the person can interpret your behavior." In other words, many common focal points are harder for autistic people to use and alternatively autistic focal points can be harder for non-autistics to use.

Schelling's original example of a focal point concerned a meeting in New York City. Let's say you agreed to meet someone there but did not specify a time or place. Schelling believed that the "focal" choice was to meet at noon beneath the main clock in Grand Central Station; in other words the focal point should be as simple and as obvious as possible. I believe that Grand Central Station was the correct choice in the 1950s and 1960s, when Schelling was promoting this idea; today, when I poll my students, I hear Ground Zero or Times Square as a focal choice more commonly.

These examples are interesting but focal points matter less today than in earlier times. It's not that the number of focal points is going down but rather that we need such focal points less. If you are supposed to meet someone in New York City, well, just send them a text message to specify where. The new focal point is not about a place but rather the expectation that you know how to read and send text messages. You can now get Google Earth on your iPhone or, if you have the right software, ask your location-tracking iPhone "Where is the nearest Starbucks from where I am standing?" The voice recognition software will do the rest and explicit knowledge substitutes for implicit knowledge. Or you can go to a new website that takes two initial locations—you enter them—and the site chooses a convenient meeting point in between. It's www.meetways.com, and if it is not famous that shows that these days focal points simply aren't such a big problem in the first place.

When it comes to picking up on commonly understood focal

points, the performance of autistics is below average in many contexts, as they find it harder to pick up on many unstated social conventions. This is one of the most common complaints you will hear or read from autistic people and it stems from the fact autistics perceive the world in different ways. But it would be wrong to conclude that autistics are incapable of having focal points. We are in fact seeing social conventions or focal points evolving among autistics, most of all with the assistance of web communication. For instance there is now a fairly common understanding, or focal point, that a meeting or goodbye among autistics will not be preceded by a handshake. Many autistics do not enjoy this form of contact, and some hate it, so why do it? There is another convention that is seeing minimal adoption among autistics but perhaps it will blossom into a more common practice. Since some autistics (albeit a minority) have difficulty recognizing peoples' faces, you should repeat your name when you say hi ("Hi, this is John"), even if you are saying hi to someone you already know.

A conversation on the phone between two autistics, or even a conversation in person, often seems slightly awkward because there is less of a common understanding of when one person is done speaking and when the other person should respond. The conversation can have an above-average number of fits, starts, and halts. On the other hand, we should not infer that autistics are in general worse at coordinating. Autistics often have a direct and even blunt style of speech and that is in my view refreshing. A preferred strategy for communicating or coordinating is simply to say what you mean, and that can do a great deal of good for communication and coordination. You also could say it is a focal point, among many self-aware autistics, not to be so offended by any perceived directness from the other person. So it's wrong to think that all the communication and coordination problems lie on the autistic side of the ledger.

The obvious question is to what extent story-based reasoning is a cognitive ability and to what extent it is also a bit of a cognitive disability. We all take the value of good stories for granted. We love to tell stories to our friends and storyteller J. K. Rowling has become a billionaire for her Harry Potter tales. At the level of research, economists insist to each other that they tell good stories in constructing their theories and offering their explanations; we commonly use the term "analytical narratives." I too love a good story, whether as a consumer of culture or professionally when I act as a consumer of economic research. But still, I'd like to raise a voice of protest. Should stories play such a dominant role in our cognition? Don't we sometimes think in terms of stories *too much?*

Let's look at how story-based thinking can go wrong and lead our lives astray, especially when the relevant stories have a highly social component. Story-based thinking, while fun, has its problematic side. I see the following problems with socially salient stories:

PROBLEM #1: THE STORIES ARE TOO SIMPLE

We've already seen that memorable stories tend to be socially salient and thus they tend to be focal. But, going back to Thomas Schelling, what do we know about focal points and the problem of how and where to meet up in New York City? We know that chosen focal points tend to be simple and obvious. That means that some of your stories will be simple and obvious as well. Some might say too simple and too obvious.

Whenever a group has to coordinate around a common idea or plan, there is the potential for what is called a least-common-denominator effect. Have you ever tried to get a group of six or eight people to agree on a common movie to go see or rent? It's hard. A lot of the best movies already have been seen by someone in the group. Or many excellent movies are in some way bizarre, offensive, or appeal to very specialized tastes. Not everyone loves the *Godfather* series (remember that horse in the bed?) and there are many reasons, whether justified or not, to object to it. Maybe one person in the group doesn't like reading subtitles on the screen. And so on. You probably won't end up with excellence; rather you'll end up with a movie that no one saw fit to veto. You'll end up with something not too offensive but probably not excellent by anyone's standard. Hollywood blockbusters have this same problem when they try to appeal to very broad audiences. They end up drained of vitality and risk-taking in an effort to appeal to the least common denominator in a large group of people, in this case spread across a truly global film audience.

We're less likely to see that the same logic applies not just to the Hollywood studios but also to ourselves. In this way I am pretty typical. Some of the inputs behind my deepest personal narratives suffer from the least-common-denominator effect. The logic applies to my dreams. To my fantasies. To my deepest visions of what I can be. I treasure those thoughts and feelings so much but in reality I pull a lot of them from a social context and I pull them from points that are socially salient. That means I pull them from celebrities, from ads, from popular culture, and most generally from ideas that are easy to communicate and disseminate to large numbers of people. We all dream in pop culture language to some degree.

Media coverage brings similar problems of oversimplification. The tendency is to fit all facts into the format of a story, usually with a memorable protagonist, even when the reality is more complex. Haven't you noticed how many movies and TV shows offer an underdog struggling against the system and receiving ultimate vindication? It makes for a good tale. Yet this isn't always the most appropriate or the most accurate way of organizing information. The media is good at portraying heroes and villains and conspiracies, while it is bad at giving people an understanding of abstract or unseen social and economic forces.

As long as we are on the topic, media coverage of autistics offers many examples of how stories—even stories intended as positive—fall into the trap of presenting easily remembered, story-based stereotypes rather than the more complex truth. A typical example is a 2008 CNN.com story about an autistic child who was very upset because the family home had burnt down from a raging fire in California. The lead idea in the story is how autistics are totally dependent on their daily routines. Just so it doesn't sound arbitrary, there is the obligatory single-sentence quotation from a scientist to justify the claim. Well, routines in autism are a complex topic but I think even the uninformed reader wonders whether such distraught feelings (the child lost all his possessions and toys and room) might be "normal" rather than "autistic." But asking that question would destroy the premise of the story, namely the notion that autistic children cannot adjust. The bombshell comes at the end of the account, when the author reveals in passing, and in unawareness of any contradiction, "'He's [the autistic boy is] doing a lot better than his mom or dad, believe it or not,' Jonathan's mother said. 'Time will tell. He's never seen anything like this.'" The reality is that the autistic boy was better at adjusting than his non-autistic parents, but emphasizing that part of the history would not produce the stereotypical, easily remembered story and so it is neglected.

CNN is of course a popular outlet and thus the story is presented in a way that many people can relate to or remember, and that means some oversimplification. In other words, the shallowness of many commonly told and commonly held stories is part of the price of our sociability and the need to share so much with so many other people. Sometimes that oversimplification is a price worth paying. But let's recognize it for what it is, namely a cognitive bias that plagues how many people think about the world.

PROBLEM #2: STORIES END UP SERVING DUAL AND CONFLICTING FUNCTIONS

Part of what a focal point means is that you can't fit too many stories, ideas, and data points into your head at once. Only some of them will stick out and be obvious or memorable. So if you think of "meeting places in New York City" a few well-known points come to mind. If your mind was flooded with all the unordered details at once, it would be harder and maybe impossible to come up with a focal locale for meeting the other person.

Just as there can only be so many focal points, so can your mind only fit or handle so many stories. Your self-narratives for what you are doing cannot be so numerous as to fill out a thirty-seven-volume encyclopedia. Instead you fill your mind with a relatively small number of stories, such as "devoted mother," "caring friend," "adventurous hiker," and so on. By the time we get to your thirtieth or even twentieth self-narrative, usually it's pretty secondary and not a major driver of your behavior.

That's fine, but the small number of focal stories does lead to some problems, namely that you don't have enough stories, or enough flexible stories, for everything you want to accomplish in life.

Let's consider a simple example. We all use stories to motivate ourselves but that means those same stories will cause us to make some mistakes. In some situations we will stay overmotivated when we ought to quit. Do you remember the wounded knight in Monty Python's Holy Grail movie who is seriously injured but is in total denial about the damage? As he loses all his limbs he yells out, "It's just a flesh wound!" and keeps on fighting, or rather he keeps on trying to fight. That flesh wound line is a pretty good self-narrative for keeping up his bravery and motivation. It's not such a good story for keeping him out of danger or for getting him to visit the doctor when needed.

You might think: "Oh, the knight just needs two stories. He can start with the bravery story and switch into the 'I am vulnerable' story when he needs to or when he starts losing the battle." But that's precisely what's not so easy. Stories need to be focal and they need to be strongly imprinted on our minds. That means we can't just jump from one story to another at will. Bravery is an overall temperament that cannot be turned on and off like a switch. Our personal stories therefore involve some "stickiness," if I may borrow some terminology from macroeconomics. The world, or our immediate environment, changes more quickly than our stories can adjust. In the meantime we can be very vulnerable indeed.

It sounds like a simple problem, but the indivisibility and stickiness of our emotional states—and thus our stories—is a root cause of so many of our life problems and a root cause of so many institutional failures. For instance, consider the collapse of the real estate bubble, as it started in 2007. Some of those mortgage lenders were fraudulent, but a lot of them just didn't see that the story of perpetually rising home prices had to come to an end and that it would come to an end as soon as it did.

The stickiness of our stories is also why, on the macroeconomic level, economies experience nasty business cycles. Much of modern macroeconomics is built around the idea that some wages and prices do not adjust downward easily. If you are fired because business is slow, you might wonder, "Why didn't they offer to keep me on for a 20 or maybe 30 percent pay cut?" Sometimes this happens but the reality is that most workers develop poor morale, or foment rebellion, when their wages are cut. You start life with the story "I will fight unfairness against me and efforts to take things away from me." That story works well in a lot of settings (including the playpen), but in the world of business it sometimes means you end up getting fired. You ought to be switching into the story "I need to take one on the chin to regroup and move on" but the reality is that most people do not make this adjustment smoothly. Even if you can make that adjustment, your employer doesn't know that about you and so you get fired instead of the pay cut. That's a big reason why the downward swing of the business cycle usually involves so much unemployment.

Thomas Schelling, in his "The Mind as a Consuming Organ," understood the very human limitations behind our stories and our limited mental and emotional capacities: "Marvelous it is that the mind does all these things. Awkward it is that it seems to be the same mind from which we expect both the richest sensations and the most austere analyses."

PROBLEM #3: MARKETS DON'T ALWAYS SEND US THE RIGHT STORIES OR REINFORCE THE RIGHT STORIES

Insofar as you open yourself, and your stories, to social influence you run the risk of external manipulation. Our choice of stories is never autonomous and the choice is never ours alone. We've already looked at how we pull our stories from others and how we choose our stories so they resonate with other people as well. That's one issue, but the more sinister reality is that other people are trying to manipulate you with stories all the time. These villains include your employer, politicians, advertisers, and who knows, maybe even some authors as well. Isn't fiction deliberately a kind of manipulation, preying on our imperfections and designed so we care about and sympathize with characters that aren't even real?

On one hand you are trying to empty your head and your feelings of a lot of extraneous clutter. You do this, in part, to keep your personal stories focal and memorable. Sadly, all these external persuaders are trying to fill your head at the same time you are trying to empty it. It's a kind of social arms race—one side against the other—and unfortunately we as individual story-builders are not always the ones who win out.

Look at capitalist advertising, where the manipulative persuasion is easiest to spot. With the goal of profit in mind, advertisers try to promote the following kinds of goods and services:

- goods we will become addicted to
- goods that are hard for competitors to copy or reproduce
- goods that the supplier can produce more of at low or declining cost

Those are the goods that are most profitable to market and sell. The direct corollary is that we will be bombarded with stories about the importance of these goods. Coke: the real thing. Finger-lickin' good (Kentucky Fried Chicken). Please don't squeeze the Charmin. And so on. In other words, you get stories that are bundled with these goods. It's the stories that help you get addicted to these goods and to their associated images.

As I've noted, addiction isn't always a bad thing, especially if you're having fun and the habit isn't destructive. If you've grown attached to eating healthy Rainier cherries (as I have, and in case you don't know, those are the yellow ones), that's fine, albeit a bit expensive. But still, the addictive goods promoted by advertisers are not exactly the best choices for you either. The world is sending you stories with a skewed perspective. Because of the influence of ads and popular culture, there is a risk that our personal narratives can become too aspirational, too commercial, and too linked to specific brands. We are also too susceptible to government propaganda.

Autistic people have some cognitive strengths to help them deal with those problems. The love of information found among autistic people meets only the first criterion on the above list, namely it may be addictive. Many ways in which autistics engage with information just don't yield that much profit to suppliers, precisely because the relevant processes of mental ordering are such cheap pleasures. Most instances of autistic mental ordering don't need to be linked to scarce and possibly expensive social status goods. The ordering is very often an extreme form of what economists call "household production" and so these pleasures cannot easily be controlled, manipulated, or owned by outside forces. That gives many autistics one kind of freedom from the pressures of commercial society.

Autistics may not seem like such a powerful group, but their techniques of information engagement embody a threat to capitalist marketing as we know it, and I mean that in the best sense. Why buy an expensive brand repeatedly when you can make your own economy in your head? As the evolution of the web illustrates, other people are catching up to this insight and producing more value by their own mental ordering and enjoying that value in their minds, without the intermediation of many expensive commodities. When it comes to protecting yourself against external manipulation by advertisers, a preoccupation with mental ordering is often an underappreciated advantage.

The Portuguese author Fernando Pessoa hit on a fundamental reality: "Wise is the man who monotonizes his existence, for then each minor incident seems a marvel. A hunter of lions feels no adventure after the third lion. For my monotonous cook, a fist-fight on the street always has something of a modest apocalypse . . . The man who has journeyed all over the world can't find any novelty in five thousand miles, for he finds only new things—yet another novelty, the old routine of the forever new—while his abstract concept of novelty got lost at sea after the second new thing he saw." Pessoa calls this "monotonizing existence, so that it won't be monotonous. Making daily life anodyne, so that the littlest thing will amuse." Pessoa may be overstating the point, but this is one strategy that stands outside of most capitalist marketing.

The competitive pressures from free fun on the web affect the marketing prospects for virtually all goods and services, again because there is competition. If you're trying to addict me to drinking expensive bottles of red wine, such a habit now has some especially cheap competition, again as can be found on the web. And no, it's not just the web that is changing the terms of the competition in favor of cheap pleasures. TiVo makes it easy to obsess over basketball and cable TV means that your favorite TV show can be suited to your particular interests in a very intense way.

But aren't stories really just fantasy and isn't just "living in your head," when you get right down to it, simply bad? There is a fundamental criticism that must be addressed.

The criticism comes from Robert Nozick, the former Harvard philosopher, who provided what is considered the strongest and most potent critique of stories and fantasy. Nozick was an especially imaginative man and like so many other philosophers he wanted to convince us that there is something special about authenticity. (Recall Heidegger, or for that matter Sartre's *Nausea:* "But you have to choose: to live or to recount.") Toward that end, he poses what has now become a famous philosophical challenge, namely that of the experience machine, which he outlined in his 1974 book *Anarchy, State, and Utopia.*

The experience machine, as Nozick called it, offers the promise of experiencing whatever we want to. We could live our lives as heroes, have a hundred beautiful boyfriends or girlfriends, cure all of the world's diseases, or be the world's richest or most athletic man. It's a bit like the movie *Total Recall* except there is no malfunction and no evil corporation lurking in the background. It's just us and the pure fulfillment of all of our dearest dreams. You just have to plug into the machine, and of course the catch is that none of these experienced events are real. Once you are plugged in you think they are real (but only if you want to); in reality you are in a stinky room, lying on a dirty cot and hooked up to an ugly machine. Maybe there's a worm crawling up your leg or maybe you're in a clean, white hospital bed. You'll never know.

Nozick claims that most of us will reject such a fate, even though it provides us with some extraordinary mental experiences. For Nozick the rejection of the experience machine establishes a few philosophical points. First, we want to be certain kinds of persons, not just receptacles of happiness. Second, we value the truth or the authenticity of an experience. Third, hedonism cannot be the only or primary value because if it was we would all plug into the machine. Fourth, the meaning of humanity can't just be all about "living in our heads."

But I'm not quite convinced by Nozick's critique, even though I largely agree with the four points listed immediately above. Perhaps my skepticism stems from my background as an economist and my profession's emphasis on "choice at the margin," to cite that theme again. The choice is not "Fantasy: yes or no?" but rather "How much fantasy do we want in our lives?"

I've decided to plug into an experience machine, or at least not to unplug, and that machine is the human mind. It's pretty well established that our minds shape and frame truth as much as track it and few people would want, upon reflection, to live a life unadorned by the power of framing effects. We use framing effects all the time to make our experiences more vivid and more intense. Nor would most people, upon reflection, want a life without self-deception. If we were truly aware, all the time, of all the world's suffering, and more importantly aware fully of our own mediocrities (not to mention our inevitable death), many of us wouldn't be so happy. And as I've argued in my previous book, *Discover Your Inner Economist,* beneficial self-deception is common in human life, especially in marriage and career ambition. A lot of human achievement takes place only because we tell ourselves—often contrary to reason—that we are in fact smarter or wiser or better than other people.

In other words, we are all—now—allowing deliberately false movies to play through our heads and in part we let this happen so that we are happier and more successful. So for me the question is not whether to plug into or not plug into a machine, but rather how much to plug in and to what kind of machine. No one is choosing to opt for pure authenticity—whatever you might think that means—so let's not set up pure fantasy on the other side of the equation. It's all about choosing the right margin (again, that term from economics) of reality and fantasy, or to put it another way, I don't think the so-called real world is very "authentic" at all. No one who refuses to plug into the machine is in fact choosing or defending pure authenticity.

If it did turn out that autistics have purer or less intermediated sensory perceptions, as is suggested under some hypotheses, would everyone then prefer to be autistic? Probably not. Coming at the question from the other side, many autistic people do not wish for or seek a cure; people very often like to keep what they were born with and also what they have shaped themselves into.

That said, I can think of plenty of settings where I would opt for the experience machine, even if I would not take the machine today. Nozick wrote up the experience machine example when he was in his forties, brilliant, dashingly handsome, in the prime of his life, and tenured at Harvard with a very high salary. No wonder he didn't want to plug in. But if I had only a year left of life—let's make that two years—I'd run for the machine pretty quickly, at least if my family had already passed on. Or if I lived in the Congo, where millions have died from civil war . . . well . . . I don't know what that kind of life is really like but I'd give the machine serious consideration.

Or say you personally don't want the machine, but your acceptance will save five other people's lives. Would you proceed without guilt or reluctance? And how many lives should be needed to push you over the edge? I would think that one other life to be saved would be more than enough to accept the machine hookup. I don't think I would feel very remorseful about choosing the machine, once society made me a hero and removed the social and personal stigma of my having "voted against authenticity." I might look forward to what is to follow and if I had any worry it would simply be whether the machine was truly and properly designed for me.

So is the experience machine example compelling as a refutation of stories, fantasy, and living in your head? Is the machine truly a reaffirmation of "the real"? I don't think so, and again that's because "living in your head" is all about choice at the margin. (If you are wondering, Nozick and Schelling were at Harvard at the same time and they were admirers of each other's work; there may have been mutual influence.)

I'll do a flip on Nozick's original intentions. The question of the experience machine, properly specified and construed, puts a self-constructed mental economy squarely on the map as one value that matters and as one value that is *undervalued* in many circumstances. To be honest, many of my friends have not read *Moby-Dick* but I think many more of them should indulge in this fantasy of the quest for the white whale. That is, unless they have three small children running around the house.

Many of us are too reluctant to step (part-time) into literary fantasy machines rather than too ready. Isn't our general tendency to clutch at the thought of reality just one more instance of the illusion that we are always in control? I say let's put down our polemic against living in our heads and let's put down our bias against interiority. Let's give our stories their proper due but also recognize the limits of stories. The quality and vitality of our internal economies—and thus the quality and vitality of our society—depends on it.

7

HEROES

When it comes to stories, most of us love to read fiction but we're not always aware of why we find fiction appealing. I'm not going to tackle this question in its broadest terms but I do wish to focus on one reason why some works of fiction are so fascinating. Fiction can be a surprisingly good medium for representing the dynamism and also the subtleties of human cognition. The potential beauty, power, and nobility of mental ordering isn't some recent novelty, but rather it is an underlying theme in the history of Western ideas and I wish to show you as such. I'd also like to show you that novels and stories can offer instructive or interesting tales about the autism spectrum. This belies the common view that autism has little to do with human interaction and human emotion. The notion that "an autistic mind" can be an "entertaining mind" or an "appealing mind" is a shocking one to many people, but I believe it is true.

To dig into the topic, I will start with autism in fiction, but keep in mind these tales are also offering broader lessons about all human cognition. The writers I will consider didn't know about autism as a formal phenomenon so of course they viewed their character portraits in terms of human universals and human eccentricities rather than medical pathologies; often this makes them more rather than less insightful.

I see Sherlock Holmes as the most fully developed autistic character in the Western literary tradition. Of course Sir Arthur Conan Doyle—who died in 1930—had no scientific knowledge of the autism spectrum as a specific phenomenon. But his characterization of Sherlock Holmes fits our current understanding fairly closely, although with some exaggerations and dramatizations for the sake of the story. Doyle also portrays Holmes as having cognitive, personality, and behavioral traits from what we now call the autism spectrum and he offers a sophisticated understanding of their possible connection to the life of an individual human being, albeit a fictional one.

In case you have been living under a rock, Sherlock Holmes is a fictional London detective who solves cases by noticing very small clues and constructing elegant chains of reasoning and thereby identifying the criminal or solving some mystery. That alone may not sound decisive but from the beginning it seems that Holmes has a relationship to the autism spectrum, even though it is never described as such. From the very first Holmes story—"A Study in Scarlet"— Doyle stresses Holmes's ability to perceive small details and changes, his meticulous methods of reasoning, his apparent emotional detachment (and "apparent" is the right word), and how he loves to impose the order of his mind upon his favored areas of specialization. But it's not just about the stereotypes. While Holmes may strike the superficial reader as a cold automaton, he is a deeply engaging and charismatic character.

An especially strong interest in parts and small details is a classic trait found frequently in people along the autism spectrum; Holmes of course focuses on small telltale signs of causal relations behind crimes and other puzzles of detection. Dr. Watson describes Holmes as having "an extraordinary genius for minutae" ("The Sign of Four," p. 126; see the "Further Reading and References" section for information on the editions cited in this chapter; unless otherwise indicated I am referring to volume I of the Holmes edition). Holmes describes his own brain as comparable to an attic that has to be "stocked with furniture" ("A Study in Scarlet," p. 13) and ordered in the proper manner. Like many autistics Holmes has a phenomenal command of some facts—in his chosen or preferred areas—but he is often quite ignorant or naïve about most everything else; Watson reminds him of this discrepancy throughout the stories. In his spare time Holmes writes and publishes the definitive monograph of the polyphonic motets of Lassus, the Renaissance composer, and yet he is clueless about many other things, such as philosophy or political science. Holmes also is an asocial bachelor who never goes on a date or expresses romantic interest in women (or men).

Here are a few of the more direct passages describing Holmes:

> "My mind," he [Holmes] said, "rebels at stagnation. Give me problems, give me work, give me the most abstruse cryptograms, or the most intricate analysis, and I am in my own proper atmosphere." ["The Sign of Four," p. 124]
>
> He is not a man that it is easy to draw out, though he can be communicative enough when the fancy strikes him. ["A Study in Scarlet," p. 5]

He was quiet in his ways, and his habits were regular. ["A Study in Scarlet," p. 11]

He has the tidiest and most orderly brain, with the greatest capacity for storing facts, of any man living. ["The Adventure of the Bruce-Partington Plans," vol. 2, p. 400]

Holmes could talk exceedingly well when he chose, and that night he did choose. He appeared to be in a state of nervous exaltation. I have never known him so brilliant. He spoke on a quick succession of subjects—on miracle plays, on medieval pottery, on Stradivarius violins, on the Buddhism of Ceylon, and on the warships of the future—handling each as though he had made a special study of it. ["The Sign of Four," p. 197]

"I was never a very sociable fellow, Watson, always rather fond of moping in my rooms and working out my own little methods of thought, so that I never mixed much with the men of my year." ["The 'Gloria Scott,'" p. 585]

Sherlock Holmes had, in a very remarkable degree, the power of detaching his mind at will. For two hours the strange business in which we had been involved appeared to be forgotten, and he was entirely absorbed in the pictures of the modern Belgian masters. He would talk of nothing but art . . . ["Three Broken Threads," vol. 2, p. 39]

We also learn that he reads ciphers easily ("The Warning," vol. 2, p. 165), he dislikes publicity ("The Adventure of the Devil's Foot," vol. 2, p. 465), and he has "an abnormally acute set of senses," including an acutely sensitive sense of smell ("The Adventure of the Blanched Soldier," vol. 2, p. 551), again all tendencies associated, to varying degrees, with those on the autism spectrum.

Personally, I got the biggest kick out of the description of how Holmes organizes his physical space:

> Although in his methods of thought he was the neatest and most methodical of mankind, and although also he affected a certain quiet primness of dress, he was none the less in his personal habits one of the most untidy men that ever drove a fellow-lodger to distraction . . . month after month his papers accumulated until every corner of the room was stacked with bundles of manuscripts which were on no account to be burned and which could not be put away save by their owner. ["The Musgrave Ritual," pp. 604–5]

Maybe those passages, taken alone, are not fully convincing. Maybe Doyle just had some unusual personality and behavior traits in mind and he embellished them to make a good story. The real clincher, in my view, comes in the story "The Greek Interpreter," where Watson finally meets Holmes's brother, Mycroft.

In the early part of the story Holmes relates to Watson that he knows his unusual talents are hereditary and he knows this because those same talents can be found in his brother, only much more strongly. Holmes describes his brother Mycroft as his "superior in observation and deduction." Mycroft also has "an extraordinary faculty for figures." In a later story Mycroft is described as having "the tidiest and most orderly brain, with the greatest capacity for storing facts, of any man living" ("The Adventure of the Bruce-Partington Plans," vol. 2, p. 400). Mycroft, however, is portrayed as incapable of detective work, although sometimes he helps audit the books for government departments.

Mycroft also belongs to something called the Diogenes Club, which has "the most unsociable and most unclubable men in town" ("The Greek Interpreter," p. 684); the club is so asocial that even Holmes does not seem to belong. As Doyle describes it, the members are either misanthropes or shy. Furthermore the club members are not allowed to notice each other, save for one room where talking is permitted. Repeated violations will lead to expulsion from the club. When I read this I thought of Autreat, the yearly conference on autism, where attendees can wear badges indicating that they do not wish to be approached or spoken to; the badges are to be taken seriously.

The reader does get to meet Mycroft, who turns out to speak in very dispassionate terms, far more so than Holmes, and of course all of Mycroft's deductive surmises turn out to be correct. Mycroft easily bests Holmes at reasoning but at the end of the day Mycroft has retreated back into his private world and Holmes is off to solve his next case.

Mycroft appears again in the tale "The Adventure of the Bruce-Partington Plans." In this story it turns out that Mycroft works as a personal, individualized information clearinghouse for the government of England. When ministers have queries they come to Mycroft and he responds with all the relevant information, serving as a kind of human Google and seeing all possible interconnections across policy areas and the body of human knowledge. Mycroft at first appears quite unable to get much done but in reality some of his specialized talents are extremely practical and useful ones. Mycroft is also described as a man of rigid habits. Furthermore he realizes that he is not up to the work of Holmes, as he states that running around to "cross-question railway guards" is not his comparative advantage ("Bruce-Partington Plans," vol. 2, p. 404). It's pretty clear that Doyle saw the characters of Sherlock and Mycroft Holmes as stemming from the programming of their minds.

The other potentially autistic character in the stories is Holmes's mirror enemy, Professor Moriarty. Moriarty is "endowed by nature with a phenomenal mathematical faculty" ("The Final Problem," p. 739) and he has authored a book on the mathematical dynamics of asteroids ("The Warning," vol. 2, p. 164). When it comes to deduction he is exactly the equal of Holmes. We are told, "He sits motionless, like a spider in the centre of its web, but that web has a thousand radiations, and he knows well every quiver of them" (p. 740). To drive home the notion of similarity, when Moriarty finally meets Holmes, the evil man utters the classic line "All that I have to say has already crossed your mind."

Obviously the idea of judging a fictional character as anything not intended by the author is a problematic one. There is no fact of the matter as to whether Moriarty "is autistic" because, among other reasons, Moriarty is not even a real person. Furthermore famous literary characters tend to come off to us, once they become famous, as a set of clichés of their own making. So the point is not any tight identification of the autism spectrum across the worlds of fiction and nonfiction, but simply to point out how much the stories deal with what I have called the cognitive strengths of the autism spectrum.

Holmes is a hero but there is also a critique of Holmes's life embedded in these stories. Doyle describes Holmes as "cold" ("A Scandal in Bohemia," p. 239) and we are told on occasion that Holmes is a drug user, specifically of morphine and cocaine. At the time this description was not intended as the horror it might seem today; the harms of these drugs were not fully understood and they did not face the social and legal sanctions that were later imposed. But still the impression is that Holmes, while not a heavy user, takes the drugs to fill the emptiness of his life. If we think of Holmes as performing his own "cultural self-assembly," he takes in pure analysis (detection) and pure pleasure (the drugs) but in separate form. There is never much real integration of pleasure or life experience. Doyle is suggesting that Holmes's way of life is unsatisfying and unable to provide for many of the best and most fulfilling sides of human existence; if you'd like a happier interpretation Watson later relates (in "The Adventure of the Missing Three-Quarter") that Holmes gave up drugs at his urging.

This description of Holmes might remind you a bit of the television character Gregory House, the brilliant doctor played by Hugh Laurie in the television series *House M.D.* Like Holmes, House has extraordinary powers of detection, which he presents to the world in the form of monologues. House solves cases that no one else can, yet he is also addicted to painkillers. He speaks very bluntly, he is a nonconformist, and at one point in the series it is speculated that he might be well-described by Asperger's. I believe that Gregory House, as a character, is very much patterned after Sherlock Holmes.

In any case, what's so striking and insightful about Doyle's stories (and *House*'s, for that matter) is that Holmes is not merely painted as an asocial, weird misfit. Doyle, without even knowing about autism, both presents and then goes beyond many of the standard clichés about autism.

Holmes was very much a loved character to the broader public; Doyle knew this and in fact he resented Holmes's popularity. Doyle killed Holmes off in one story, but he later had to bring him back at reader insistence; Doyle needed the sales and the money. Doyle relates that many women of the time wrote him, hoping either to keep house for Holmes or to marry him; to these readers Holmes was a very real and indeed an attractive figure. The Sherlock Holmes figure inspires readers and fans to this day and there are more than four hundred Sherlock Holmes societies around the world, even though the details of Doyle's mysteries might seem musty to many contemporary readers. There's still a regular flow of correspondence to Holmes at 221B Baker Street—his address in the stories—and the company holding that address had to appoint a permanent secretary to deal with the flow of mail.

It's really the characters—most of all Holmes—that have made the stories stand up over time. Sherlock Holmes arguably can be considered the most famous single literary character in the modern Western tradition, or at the very least he stands in the top tier of such fame. He's also inspired a slew of movies and theatrical adaptations. That's a striking achievement for a character type that many people stereotype as unattractive or less than human. No one is laughing when Watson, upon hearing of the apparent death of Holmes, describes him as "the best and wisest man whom I have ever known" ("The Final Problem," p. 755). Doyle knew it wasn't enough to call Holmes impressive or smart, although of course those qualities described him too. Holmes has a deep perspective on human society that the other people in the stories simply do not. It's interesting that when Holmes has two years of forced retirement (he needs to hide from men trying to kill him), he goes to visit the Dalai Lama in Tibet to refresh his mind.

So what in the Holmes portrait makes him likable and also so very human? First is Holmes's loyalty to Watson and his love of their time together. He is low-key when Watson comes to visit him but his enjoyment of the experience and of the camaraderie is palpable. Second is Holmes's total involvement in what he does, which makes him a man of charisma. Third is Holmes's powerful intuition. For all of Doyle's talk of deduction, Holmes isn't very deductive or for that matter very scientific at all. If you read through his "deductions" with even a small amount of care, you will see that they are often questionable as purely formal surmises or sometimes even arrant nonsense. This looseness can be seen as a feature of the stories rather than a bug. Most of all Holmes is a man of remarkable intuition about other human beings. He's very far from being a calculating machine but he is able to see many things that others do not and he can grasp their implications in surprising ways.

In other words he is often able to see the big picture and not just the small details that comprise it. Consistent with this portrait, the ability of autistics to engage in big-picture thinking—albeit in sometimes specialized or different ways—is a theme in recent cognitive research.

Some logicians, and also the author and semiotics expert Umberto Eco, have described Holmes's reasoning as a form of "abduction"—stabbing in the dark to postulate what may be the case—rather than deduction in the formal sense. A big part of Holmes's appeal is simply how much he is opposed to conventional patterns of thought and the ordinary presuppositions of society. Michael Atkinson wrote of Holmes's "fresh and scrupulous attention" to "the apparently insignificant."

It's also striking just how much of the action in the stories takes place between the personalities. In fact, very often Holmes doesn't catch the criminal at all, even though he usually figures out some aspect of the puzzle. If you're looking for suspense, most of the action is found in the interior dimension and not in scenes of chase or confrontation.

Watson, of course, loves Holmes, and anyone who has read the stories probably knows I don't mean this in a romantic or sexual sense; indeed it is striking how easily the stories avoid gay or homoerotic interpretations. Watson is strongly attracted to Holmes's passion and commitment, in addition to being intrigued by his cognitive abilities. For a while Watson marries and drifts away from Holmes, spending much less time with him. But Watson is repeatedly drawn back to Holmes and eventually Holmes proves to be a more suitable regular companion than does Watson's wife. Exactly what happens to Watson's wife is unclear but Watson ends up moving back in with Holmes ("The Adventure of the Norwood Builder") despite his medical practice. It is not obvious that Watson needs to split the rent but of course readers wanted to see the pair reunited. Given the magnetism of Holmes, the reader feels it is right that the two men should be spending so much of their time together.

The standard reading of the stories is to see Watson as an opposite of Holmes or as a foil to showcase Holmes's extremes. But a deeper reading shows it isn't so simple and that the complexity of the character of Watson helps make the portrait of Holmes both more realistic and more sympathetic.

For one thing, Watson learns how to mimic Holmes. Watson had long been an astute observer himself but not of crimes. Watson's powers of observation and memory are showcased whenever a woman enters the scene in one of the stories. He notices just about everything about her, most of all her manner, her charm, and her mode of dress. Had the topic of the observation not been a woman, a reader might almost have been mistaken in thinking that it was Holmes offering the analysis. Here's a typical passage (from "The Adventure of the Beryl Coronet," pp. 479–480):

> A young lady came in. She was rather above the middle height, slim, with dark hair and eyes, which seemed the darker against the absolute pallor of her skin. I do not think I have ever seen such deadly paleness in a woman's face. Her lips, too, were bloodless, but her eyes were flushed with crying. As she swept silently into the room she impressed me with a greater sense of grief than the banker had done in the morning, and it was the more striking in her as she was evidently a woman of strong character, with immense capacity for self-restraint.

Watson is in general obsessed with understanding faces and in particular eyes. Another typical passage is this:

> Douglas was a remarkable man, both in character and in person. In age he may have been about fifty, with a strong-jawed, rugged face, a grizzling moustache, peculiarly keen gray

eyes, and a wiry vigorous figure which had lost nothing of the strength and activity of youth. He was cheery and genial to all, but somewhat offhand in his manners, giving the impression that he had seen life in social strata on some far lower horizon than the country society of Sussex. ["The Tragedy of Birlstone," vol. 2, p. 181]

Holmes, in contrast, derives his deductions from just about everywhere but the face. He examines the soot on the collar, the condition of the fingers, the mud on the boots, the condition of the clothes, the initials on the lapel, and many other physical characteristics, but he draws very few conclusions from the countenance.

It is easy to think of Holmes as the analytical one, but as the stories progress Watson reveals a growing albeit halting tendency toward some of Holmes's behavioral traits. While Holmes collects information in a very obvious way, eventually it dawns on us that Watson is the one preoccupied with chronicling everything that happens. This ordering of experience is revealed to be an obsession of Watson's. If Watson has any favorite pastime, it is either visiting Holmes (during the times they did not live together) or rereading his notes about his adventures with Holmes. Holmes is very pleased that Watson has organized his notes, and his accounts of the adventures, on a logical and ordered basis rather than structuring them around sensational or emotional factors ("The Adventure of the Copper Beeches," p. 492). The point is not that Doyle wanted to establish any ultimate equivalence between the personalities of Watson and Holmes, but again he showed the reader that Holmes is not so far removed from ordinary human experience.

Having read these stories, I can't help but wonder where the character of Holmes came from. It's hard to find many useful clues in the major biographies of Doyle and it is hard to get a sense of what the man was really like. It's well known that some aspects of the Holmes character came from Poe's fictional detective Dupin and also from Doyle's Edinburgh medical teacher, Dr. Joseph Bell. But I tend to think that Holmes's core elements came from Doyle himself.

Doyle, in his autobiography, when referring to Holmes, notes that an author cannot spin a character out of thin air unless the author has some possibilities of that character within himself. In 1918 Doyle once told an American journalist in a private interview: "If anyone is Holmes then I must confess it is I." Adrian Conan Doyle, in a biography he wrote of his father, described him as an extraordinary reader to the point of being freakish; he could for instance hold the contents of a book within his head for twenty years. His son often tested him and the father never failed to summon up the required knowledge. Adrian also wrote that "meeting any ex-serviceman, he could, and would, immediately inform the astounded recipient not only the name of his former brigade and division but the principal actions in which it took part." Adrian put it most succinctly: "[H]is mind was a great store-house of assimilated knowledge in a series of time-proof compartments."

Doyle and Holmes were both tall and physically strong, both loved boxing and Turkish baths, were both untidy, both had a horror of destroying documents, both were omnivorous readers, and both favored the political union of England and the United States. Both were deeply interested in heredity, ancient manuscripts, and the Cornish language. Pierre Nordon describes Holmes as one of the last defenders of chivalry in English-language literature and most of all as an advocate of the innocent and victims; that is how Doyle saw himself, given the many public campaigns he fought, such as that against colonial Belgian oppression in the Congo. The point is not that Doyle and Holmes were similar in every way but rather that Doyle was well aware of how closely he was tied to his most beloved character. It's also worth noting that none of Doyle's other works succeeded in producing any memorable characters at all, perhaps because he had used up the main source material he had, namely himself.

That's Holmes, but of course he is not the only character in the literary canon with a connection to the autism spectrum. The other prime example I have in mind is a hero as well.

The second literary portrait comes from southern Germany, specifically Hermann Hesse's *The Glass Bead Game* (*Das Glasperlenspiel* in German), first published in 1943. The story is set in an imaginary society combining elements of the past and the future but imagined by Hesse as the twenty-fifth century. Joseph Knecht, the protagonist, becomes the Magister (master) of the Glass Bead Game, which I'll explain in more detail shortly. Over time Joseph develops a deeper appreciation of the rewards and drawbacks of a life devoted to the Glass Bead Game. At the end of the novel he suddenly resigns his high-status position as Magister and, in a scene patterned after Buddhist philosophy, goes on a lone voyage of self-discovery.

The Glass Bead Game itself is deliberately portrayed as a bit mysterious, but I regard it as a stand-in for one scheme or method of mental ordering. As presented in the book, it takes years to learn the rules of the game, which are very complex and can never be grasped in their entirety. The rules are based on a "highly developed secret language drawing upon several sciences and arts, but especially mathematics and music (and/or musicology), and capable of expressing and establishing interrelationships between the content and conclusions of nearly all scholarly disciplines." Playing the Glass Bead Game is like playing an organ, but using all the ideas and values of mankind rather than musical notes. All of these ideas are reduced in the game to intellectual concepts and in theory the game can reproduce the entire intellectual content of the universe. The game uses beads rather than letters or musical notes but it isn't much of a leap to see the beads as stand-ins for information. It is fundamentally a game of symbols and at one point it is noted that the game brings mathematics and music to a common symbolic denominator. The origins of the game are to be found in Pythagoras and also among Gnostic circles, the medieval Scholastics, and Leibniz, among other sources (see the discussion of philosophy in the next chapter for more on these sources). We also learn that the game arose because people largely ceased to produce works of art and withdrew from the bustle of the world. The growing profundity of musical science, starting after 1900, was another important inspiration. Other parts of the game developed as aids to memory.

If you've made it this far in the book you can understand why I view the game as a competitive autistic enterprise writ large and elevated to high social status. Hesse's text is sometimes relegated to being an artifact of late German romanticism, or perhaps 1960s youth culture, but in reality it has never been more relevant than it is today.

The Glass Bead Game ends up as the centerpiece of culture in Joseph Knecht's world and the players of the game hold a status somewhat akin to that of a priestly caste. The game evolved from a specialized entertainment to casting its spell upon most of the intellectuals in society (p. 37). It became a sublime cult of "magic theater," taking over the roles of art, learning, and religion to large degree (pp. 38–39). It is also the case that "every active Glass Bead Game player naturally dreams of a constant expansion of the fields of the Game until they include the entire universe. Or rather, he constantly performs such expansions in his imagination and his private Games, and cherishes the secret desire for the ones which seem to prove their viability to be crowned by official acceptance" (p. 140).

For all this intellectualism, it becomes necessary to modify the game over time. Earlier versions of the game were too dependent on "ordering" and "grouping" and the game was dominated by mnemonists with "freakish memories and no other virtues." These players were able to dazzle the others "by their rapid muster of countless ideas." But over time these displays of virtuosity came under a strict ban to restore the integrity of the game. The all-important element of contemplation was introduced into the game to make it richer, less mechanical, and above all more spiritual. Meditation became part of the game's procedures and all of these new influences on the game were drawn from Eastern philosophy. This development kept the hieroglyphs of the game "from degenerating into mere empty signs" (pp. 38–39). In the language of this book, the revised version of the game integrates methods from both mental ordering and Buddhism.

Yet over time further cracks develop in the façade of the game; it seems that the integration with Eastern philosophy proved insufficient. Critics start charging that the game is a destructive substitute for the arts and that its players are dilettantes (p. 81). Eventually Joseph himself starts questioning the game, even after he has become Magister. He starts wondering whether it is really the highest form of the intellect and whether it might not be a mere form of play. He also asks himself whether the game merits his lifelong service (p. 136). At first Knecht fears that the decline of the game would bring anarchy and license upon society and so initially he clings to the game as a source of order (pp. 270–72). Yet over time Knecht's doubts return and grow. He wonders whether specialization in the game offers much of an overview of life's possibilities and he sees the game as an intellectualization that has evolved for its own sake and is no longer goal-directed (p. 349). Knecht also fears that the game will end up being seen as useless and it will lose its financial support from broader society (p. 361).

Knecht tries to debate these issues with the fellow members of his order but their views are too calcified and the discussions prove useless. Although he is the Magister and thus the leader, Joseph decides to leave the order and he sets out on a walk to experience the world. The formal part of the story concludes when he drowns in a river and his body is discovered by a shaken member of the order, who realizes that his life will never again be the same.

After the end of the formal story, the novel offers the reader the "Posthumous Writings of Joseph Knecht." The poems of his student years show that Knecht had doubts about the game from the very beginning. The volume concludes with "Three Lives," which offers three different stories of people on spiritual quests who learn from teachers; in these stories the game is nowhere to be found.

For all of the critique found in Hesse's novel, like Doyle Hesse presents a more balanced picture of his subject than might be apparent on a quick reading. Joseph, the most interesting and sympathetic character in the novel, has had his life and indeed his entire perspective shaped by the game. Joseph embodies the game in many ways and it is no accident that he, with his warmth and depth, has gone on to become Magister of the entire game structure. He is also the one supremely human character in the novel. It seems Joseph cannot survive without the game—once he leaves it he dies. The game is not just a triviality or a corruption, but rather it is an independent source of meaning and beauty. The problem arises when the game becomes a ruling principle for all of society, and indeed that is an unsustainable state of affairs because of human diversity. Throughout the story we're introduced to an entire cast of characters (most notably the rowdy Tegularius) who ultimately do not fit into the game and who cannot abide by its rules.

Many people who read the story find the descriptions of the game, and its players, to be the most exciting and compelling part of the narrative. There's a reason for that, just like there is a reason for the ongoing popularity of Sherlock Holmes. Hesse is one of those writers with a deep and balanced view, if only in fictional terms, and if only implicitly, of some important aspects of the autism spectrum.

Dare we look at biographical information about Hesse? I suspected what was coming before I cracked open the first biography on the shelf.

Before Hesse was six years old, his family sent him away, on the grounds that he was nearly uncontrollable at home. At the time his father wrote an explanation: "We are too high-strung, too weak for him, the whole family routine is not regular, not disciplined enough." It seems that Hesse had frequent meltdowns, as many children on the autistic spectrum are inclined to do. He was sent to an asylum for "retarded and epileptic" children and he was accepted there only after some pleading from his mother. Fortunately Hesse was not confined and he was allowed to study Latin and other matters. Later when he went home again he still mostly refused to talk to his family, take his medicine, or stop his tantrums. His life later calmed down and of course his fortunes turned around and he became one of Germany's greatest writers. Nonetheless for the rest of his life he sought, and then ran away from, periodic bouts of isolation.

We can't know the particular nature of Hesse's neurology nor can we diagnose him accurately from this distance in time and space. But still, his ideas in *The Glass Bead Game* seem to stem in some way from his own personal experience and it is possible that experience is related to direct experience of the autism spectrum.

The question of Hesse's life raises a more general issue about reading texts, namely how to read an author's or creator's personal history. How quickly should we conclude that various historical figures were in some way autistic, Asperger's, or neurodiverse? (Or, in other words, how much should we be willing to play Sherlock Holmes?) As you may know, there is a small cottage industry of writings devoted to these questions. If you're wondering, a typical list of historical figures claimed to be on the autism spectrum includes Hans Christian Andersen, Lewis Carroll, Herman Melville, George Orwell, Jonathan Swift, William Butler Yeats, James Joyce, Bela Bartók, Bob Dylan, Glenn Gould, Vincent van Gogh, Andy Warhol, Mozart, Gregor Mendel, Charles Darwin, Ludwig Wittgenstein, Henry Cavendish, Samuel Johnson, Albert Einstein, Alan Turing, Paul Dirac, Emily Dickinson, Michelangelo, Bertrand Russell, Thomas Jefferson, Thomas Edison, Nikola Tesla, Isaac Newton, and Willard Van Orman Quine, among others.

When it comes to any individual life, I have my worries about making any firm judgments. First, for some of these lives I know a bit about, such as Mozart's, I just don't see the evidence for autism. Mozart for instance may well have been neurodiverse in the broad sense of the word (arguably an ordinary mind could not have composed his extraordinary music) but that's not the same as placing him on the autism spectrum.

But my worry runs deeper than my skepticism about any single case. A lot of the historical diagnoses tend to focus our attention on personality and overt behavior rather than cognitive abilities and disabilities. That emphasis can be misleading, as I've argued. Maybe quite a few of the names on that list would likely qualify as connected to the autism spectrum; nonetheless I am promoting the idea of autistic cognitive strengths, not diagnosing *people*. We've had far too much of diagnosis and far too little of simply considering what keen, specialized perception and mental ordering bring to society as a whole.

Quite possibly Alan Turing and Glenn Gould were on the autism spectrum and you'll find some evidence for this in their biographies. Peter Ostwald, a psychiatrist and also a former friend of Gould's, wrote a whole book outlining the evidence, which includes Gould's unusual and demanding routines. In other words, Gould had some of the more visible features associated with the autism spectrum. Nonetheless the deeper and more important point is how many high achievers on the autism spectrum may not have left much of a historical record or continue to work undetected today. What can we learn from those people and their hidden cultural force?

I recently reread Adam Smith's *The Theory of Moral Sentiments* (or *TMS*, from 1759), a book that I had not picked up for about ten years, certainly not since I started thinking seriously about autism. *TMS* is about how we perceive the feelings of others and how we order our own minds to achieve happiness. (Most people don't do either especially well.) Smith starts with the idea of sympathy—our ability to put ourselves in the shoes of another—and lays out a highly ordered account of the biases of human nature and the tragedy of the human condition, namely our reliance on fortune, our enslavement to the opinions of others, and our inability to stop thirsting after that which we do not have. It is reputed that Smith considered *The Theory of Moral Sentiments* to be a much superior work to his *Wealth of Nations,* arguably the founding work of economic science.

This time around, reading *TMS* was a revelation, or so it seemed to me. Most of all I was stunned by how many of the elements in Smith's discourse seemed relevant to the autism spectrum. Rightly or wrongly, that's what ran through my mind the whole time I was rereading the book.

Smith's life does fit some of the patterns that you see popping up in discussions of historical figures and autism and Asperger's. He never married, he worked very diligently on focused intellectual problems, and his contemporaries described him as eccentric and absentminded. According to reports he frequently swayed his head side to side and he commonly would blurt out exactly what he thought, without much regard for the audience or its feelings. Dugald Stewart claimed that Smith had amazing powers of concentration, memory, and focus. None of that proves anything but it did not put my speculation to rest. I've also read that Smith very often talked to himself;

this has led some commentators to wonder if he had a mild form of Tourette's or some version of echolalia (the practice of repeating words and phrases heard from others; it is common in autism but by no means restricted to autistics).

Henry Mackenzie, a contemporary of Smith's, wrote: "With a most retentive memory, his conversation was solid beyond that of any man. I have often told him after half an hour's conversation, 'Sir, you have said enough to make a book.'" Dugald Stewart noted that Smith rarely initiated a topic of conversation but had a remarkably accurate memory for "trifling particulars." James Boswell described Smith's talk as coming from "a mind crowded with all manner of subjects." John Rae, who wrote the classic biography of Smith, wrote: "His voice seems to have been harsh, his utterance often stammering, and his manner, especially among strangers, often embarrassed, but many writers speak of the remarkable animation of his features as he warmed to his subject, and of the peculiar radiancy of his smile."

Or take this account of Dugald Stewart's: "He [Smith] did not fall in easily with the common dialogue of conversation, and . . . he was somewhat apt to convey his own ideas in the form of a lecture."

If you are familiar with the literature on Asperger perseverations, as they are now called, you will recognize every feature of these descriptions of Smith as corresponding to contemporary accounts of perseverations. It's as if the biographers and commentators were trying to caricature Smith, but of course they had no knowledge of the later discussions of these topics.

What's so interesting is how much insight into human personality Smith offers. He is hardly "mind blind" and *TMS* serves up many nuggets of psychological insight: "He is happiest who advances more gradually to greatness." Or: "It is often more mortifying to appear in public under small disasters, than under great misfortunes." Or: "It is the loss of this easy empire over the affections of mankind which renders the fall from greatness so insupportable."

The sections on sympathy strike me as written by a brilliant man who could only understand the concept, as it is practiced in the society of his time, by observing and classifying it in every manner possible. I often felt, while reading, that Smith had no typical understanding of sympathy but rather came to terms with the concept through a very careful observation of others. It's an outsider's view and that is why it is so perceptive. It's as if Smith felt he had to understand sympathy to survive in the world and so he studied it more intensely than any person had before him. Note also that Smith wrote down many observations about sympathy but he doesn't seem to show an intuitive understanding of which points are brilliant insights and which are ordinary observations shared by every man on the street.

When thinking about Smith, I am struck by Jared Blackburn's web discussion of the autistic theory of mind. Jared is a self-described autistic and he opined that many autistic people obtain exceptional insight into others by drawing upon their cognitive skills and approaching the topic of other people from different angles. Even if autistics have slower response speeds in understanding non-autistics, their understanding is not necessarily inferior and it may in some regards be superior.

Smith is not interested in sympathy alone but rather he also stresses how interactions with strangers bring about more objective forms of behavior and move society toward a greater emphasis on rules. Parents for instance are too indulgent with their children and most people behave too loosely with their friends. It is only with some amount of distance that we develop objectivity and most of all it is strangers who help us develop self-command and an objective sense of the virtuous. Modern commercial society, in Smith's view, is well-suited for helping to create this necessary sense of distance among people.

So was Smith autistic in the sense discussed in this book or might he fit other descriptions of Asperger's or neurodiverse? The correct answer is "I don't know and neither do you." The bigger specific lesson is that you don't have to see people on the autism spectrum as "the other." The more general lesson is to read texts, whether the text of a Sherlock Holmes story or the text of intellectual history, with a sensitivity to the uniqueness of the individual and the fundamental principles that guide that person or character's actions. For instance whether or not Smith has a relationship to the autism spectrum, that ambiguity, and the accompanying need for embrace and tolerance, is more important than whatever judgment you might end up passing on his neurology.

If you're looking to create your own economy, literature is one good place to pick up inspiration and heroes. You'll find some characters who love information in deep and interesting ways. It's common to think that an "age of Google" is eclipsing the literary classics, but a closer look shows we still can learn from plain, good ol'-fashioned books. Technology and the web can make our lives richer, but they are hardly the only places to look for important and indeed revolutionary cultural ideas.

8

BEAUTY ISN'T WHAT YOU THINK IT IS

What do you think is beautiful? If beauty isn't all that matters, it is surely something valuable that you want in your own economy. We often achieve new insights into beauty by trying on the aesthetic perspectives of other people. So let's start with one such person and then consider the lessons for our own lives.

Kiriana Cowansage, a neuroscientist in her midtwenties, is considered a very attractive and enthusiastic young woman. Her biggest enthusiasm, at least professionally, is science. She has been deeply interested in science and science-related themes since the age of four and now she is earning a doctorate in neuroscience, studying the biochemical basis for individual differences in fear expression.

My interest is not in Kiriana's science but rather in her approach to aesthetics—questions about what we find beautiful, compelling, or otherwise stimulating in a deep and fundamental way. People so often disagree about aesthetics, but Kiriana's thoughts have helped me understand why these clashes of opinion are so persistent and so hard to adjudicate through rational discussion. It also has helped me see how much hidden beauty we can find in today's world. When it comes to appreciating beauty, differences in cognition can be fundamental and if we pursue this insight consistently we will be led down some surprising paths.

In an email Kiriana wrote to me: "I'm very visually oriented, and in both literature and art, I prefer work that depicts (or evokes) realistic, concrete, high-contrast images." On fiction, Kiriana noticed: "I almost always choose plot-driven books that evoke strong, distinct, believable mental images over those that are blurry, fantastical or character-driven." Kiriana explains these tastes as, in part, driven by a need for strong stimuli.

A portrait of Kiriana in *Psychology Today* discussed some of her literary tastes, while describing her in terms of Asperger's syndrome. It was that article that first drew my attention to Kiriana. That piece quoted her, somewhat misleadingly, as follows:

> "I was partly drawn to [stories of] serial killers because of my interest in patterns, logical induction, and puzzle solving," she remembers. "These twisted individuals took puzzles to a whole new level of interest." Captivated by the process of piecing together an event based on its physical trace, she fell asleep each night trying to come up with the "perfect crime," one that could not be reconstructed.

The article caricatured Kiriana and her aesthetic emotions through an overly garish lens. It quoted her as follows: "All my obsessions related to something profoundly catastrophic . . . I have a really hard time feeling emotionally aroused. Brutal, violent, scary things were interesting to me because that was the best way to feel something." The article continued, "Her repeated readings of Bret Easton Ellis' *American Psycho* soon surpassed those of *The Wonderful World of Prehistoric Animals*."

Rather than viewing Kiriana as someone who is different and thus weird, I am more inclined to understand her as an individual whose cognition gives her special insight into aesthetics. After I read the *Psychology Today* article, I followed up with a query and Kiriana offered some explanation, revealing a more subtle picture of her tastes: "I also like art that is detail-oriented like [Edward] Gorey, who uses subtle features to cast a sinister, unnerving veil over bleak or banal snapshots. I find it interesting to mentally extract the elements that make his drawings effective. I'm similarly fascinated by Escher."

When I queried her about violence in art, Kiriana's response indicated the article was off base: "It doesn't need to be violent, it's just that violence is often portrayed with a graphical candor or bluntness that I find appealing." She says it is the realism and the puzzles of "slasher" novels that she likes, not necessarily the gore. I would add that a preference for violence and catastrophe in art is common, as evidenced by any James Bond movie or by Shakespeare's *King Lear*. Kiriana's description of her artistic tastes, and the need to be emotionally aroused, was not meant as a broader statement about the quality of her life.

From this short episode we can read off two lessons about cognition and taste. First, if we see a difference in taste we should wonder where it comes from and try to understand it, not frame it as weird. Neurology does matter for our taste in art, music, and books. The connection between neurology and taste is often easiest to detect in individuals with extreme and specialized cognitive profiles; that makes those individuals valuable beacons for spotting new insights into beauty.

We should drop many of our presuppositions about "low-quality" or "depraved" artistic tastes. When people have tastes that are different from ours, maybe they are perceiving and experiencing something that we do not. Or maybe they are not blinded by something filling our eyes and ears or by our automatic cognitive "editors."

By the way, it's not the case that all or even most people on the autism spectrum "like the same things." All human beings, including those on the autism spectrum, have areas of lesser or greater sensitivity to particular kinds of stimuli. For instance Kiriana does not always want a stronger or more brutal sensation. She reports that other times her tastes show an extreme sensitivity or aversion to some kinds of stimuli. She cannot stand bitter tastes in food and drink and for that reason she has a strong dislike of coffee. When she walks down the street she finds the noise and the sounds disturbing, so she often wears headphones to keep out or regulate those noises. The more insightful portrait of her aesthetic sense is that of a person who has unusual sensitivities to (some) aesthetic stimuli and thus unusual insights into aesthetics.

Unusual variations in perceptual abilities, as is found in autistics, lead to unusual patterns of consumption and, relative to non-autistics, greater specialization in consumption, including cultural consumption. It's easier for an autistic to receive steady or even increasing returns from a single aesthetic pursuit, if only because the autistic can notice so many small details and order the observed information so powerfully. More generally, if a person is especially good at enjoying music but below average at enjoying stories, he won't consume the typical (non-autistic) bundle of music and stories. He'll prefer more music and fewer stories and thus his patterns of cultural consumption will appear atypical.

The general tendency in the economics of culture, and also in the sociology of culture, is to look to education and social status for clues about what books, movies, music, etc. people will like and dislike. People who belong to expensive country clubs may be reluctant to indulge or even develop a taste for professional wrestling, a relatively low-status genre among their peers. Or people will buy expensive books to put on their coffee table, even if they never read them. The classic statement of this approach comes in Pierre Bourdieu's book *Distinction,* published in 1984, which looks at the connection between culture and social stratification in postwar France. Bourdieu's work is useful, but sociology can explain only so much of cultural consumption. The diverse neurologies of individual human beings drive much of the diversity behind the rich cultural menu available today.

The eighteenth-century Scottish philosopher David Hume understood the importance of the individuality of perception for our understanding of beauty. In his famous 1757 essay "Of the Standard of Taste," Hume (drawing upon John Locke and others) argued that many aesthetic disagreements stem from our differing abilities to perceive fine distinctions. For instance some people can sense a small change in a flavor and others cannot. In prescient fashion, Hume suggests that too fine an ability to perceive (again, he gives the example of tasting food) can be as much a burden as a blessing. This notion of delicacy of taste, or lack thereof, was a common theme in eighteenth-century writings on aesthetics, although it was not tied to much of an understanding of human neurology.

I've noticed that many art lovers are reluctant to "reduce" aesthetic preferences to neurology, because they feel something uniquely mysterious or something human is lost when we think too hard about the underlying science. The invocation of neurology somehow communicates a sense of cold determinism and a beauty that is distant at best. But rest assured, with or without neurology the mysteries of art largely remain. In fact a look at art through the lens of neurology can open our eyes to greater artistic mysteries and additional founts of creativity. Neurological approaches to understanding art, compared to sociological approaches, are more likely to imply art is fun and they are more likely to imply that artistic pleasures are deeply and fundamentally human.

Our particular neurology doesn't lock us into a particular set of artistic tastes. Individuals can learn to appreciate the cognitive skills and also the aesthetic perspectives of others, but first they need to know something is there to be appreciated. They need to know that strange and different kinds of music are not just a lot of phoney baloney. Sociological approaches to cultural taste often imply that taste differences are contrived, artificial, or reflect wasteful status-seeking. The result is that we appreciate taste differences less than we might and we become less curious. Neurological approaches imply that different individuals perceive different cultural mysteries and beauties. You can't always cross the gap to understand the other person's point of view, but at the very least you know something is there worth pursuing.

Writing as an admirer of Hume on many issues, including the

neurological foundations of taste, I'd like to challenge you with some conundrums on beauty and excitement, first involving music.

Our enjoyment of music, including classical music, depends fundamentally on how we perceive sounds, and that depends on our neurologies and also upon our previous listening histories. Consider the cases of people who, due to a stroke or brain injury, lose their ability to talk but not their ability to sing. Oliver Sacks, in his book *Musicophilia*, describes a man who was struck by lightning and was suddenly inspired to become a pianist (at age forty-two); "Williams syndrome" children, who are often hypermusical by nature; as well as people who find the sound of a symphony orchestra to resemble the sound of clashing pots and pans and a man who has a long-term memory primarily for music. These are exceptional cases but they illustrate the more general point—true for all human beings—that the appreciation of music depends upon individual neurologies.

We're all reliant on our faculties to convert a Nina Simone song into a pleasurable or stimulating experience, or not. There is even a group of people with a condition known as amusia. These people don't have any deficits of hearing or any signs of brain damage, yet they simply cannot find pleasure in music. In laboratory tests amusics, as they are called, cannot very well process pitch in a musical context and in this regard they have a cognitive disability. The best-known amusics in history are Che Guevara, Sigmund Freud, and the Nobel Prize–winning economist Milton Friedman. These individuals, despite their formidable intellectual strengths, never grasped the structure behind a musical scale. Amusics typically have less white matter in the right inferior frontal cortex and one explanation is that amusia follows from "impoverished communication in a right, or perhaps bilateral, temporo-frontal neural network."

Temple Grandin, who is autistic, also reports that she is not moved by music, but most amusics are not autistic. For that matter, most autistics have good abilities to perceive emotional "affect" in music. If anything, autistics seem to have an especially intense preoccupation with music. These musical interests may stem from cognitive advantages. When it comes to laboratory tests, autistics have above-average pitch perception abilities, there is a disproportionately high subgroup of autistics with perfect pitch, and autistics have above-average abilities to disaggregate the particular tones in a musical chord. It is likely that these differences are not accidents but rather are indicators of other harder-to-measure cognitive advantages in appreciating music. So we shouldn't be surprised if autistics often obsess over music or have unusual or highly specialized musical tastes.

If we are willing to use the prevailing language and standards of the scientific literature, it could be said that non-autistics have systematic cognitive deficits when it comes to music. "Being normal," as that concept is sometimes bandied about, may in fact hinder one's ability to love and appreciate music. I was intrigued by one study of this question; it found that 46 percent of those classified as having "perfect pitch" would score as "socially eccentric," as compared to 15 percent of the control group.

Tim Page, a Pulitzer Prize–winning music critic (originally for *The Washington Post*; he now teaches at USC), has been diagnosed in terms of Asperger's. He is another example of autistic strengths in music appreciation and he explains his relationship to music as follows: "'Music was not something I had to learn about from middle C,'

Page said. 'I knew about it intrinsically from the moment I heard it and needed to learn how to deal with that, how to put that together. There's no doubt that it had something to do with [Asperger's] because I was extraordinarily sensitive to music from the time I was two or three. After that, I just inhaled it.'"

Hikari Oe, one of Japan's leading contemporary composers (and son of the Nobel-winning novelist Kenzaburo Oe), is considered autistic. Oe does not see well, he has poor coordination, he cannot live on his own, and he doesn't talk very much, but he is very good at composing. He has absolute perfect pitch as well as an incredible musical memory; he can recognize any of Mozart's six-hundred-plus pieces from hearing just a few notes. His music, originally inspired by birdsong and by Mozart, has made him a celebrity in Japan and brought him several times to the top of the country's classical charts. By the way, when Hikari Oe was born he had evident brain and other medical problems; Japanese doctors tried to convince his father to let him die but his father refused, and Hikari subsequently ended up serving as an inspiration for much of his father's fiction.

Hikari Oe's music is not very "sophisticated" by many contemporary standards but it has a directness, sweetness, and naturalness that resonate with millions of listeners. The music is accessible and if anything the core language comes from Mozart. Few contemporary composers could build upon Mozart's style without affectation or excess self-consciousness. Maybe it's because I know where it came from, but when I hear Oe's music—which I enjoy—I think of the very direct manner in which many autistic people conduct their conversations.

Is Oe simply a beautiful composer? Or is he better thought of as an "autistic composer"?

One music critic, Jamie James, rebelled against the entire aesthetic behind the music. In full awareness of Oe's autism, he wrote:

> I hate this music . . . I find it completely suspect. It seems to me to have no emotional content at all. It's like music written by a schizophrenic trying to imitate the emotional state of a well person, music that intends to be happy rather than expressing a real emotional state . . . There are no surprises here. And I hate the performance, too, it's extremely metronomic, but I don't know how else you could play this, and I don't think any performance could change my mind about the music.

Maybe James is being excessively nasty or intolerant, but he does recognize that Oe offers a very distinct musical language and that the language is not for everyone. James is right that Oe's music does sound very different, and it's one more example of how aesthetic perspective depends on the neurology of the individual human mind.

OK, now let's consider a perspective on music from yet another direction. Remember atonal music, that brilliant innovation that culminated in the twentieth century? What became of it? Well, it's alive and well in the heads of many of the neurodiverse, and I mean "neurodiverse" in the broad sense of the term, not just to refer to the autism spectrum. That's right, there are some people who love this music; I think many of them have different neurological programming and that is why they are so receptive to these unusual sounds.

When the atonal works of Schoenberg and Webern first appeared, many critics believed that after some time they would be embraced as popular music. Not popular in the Top 40 sense, but popular in the sense that Mahler, Elgar, and Debussy inspire musical love in many nonprofessional listeners. Mozart and Chopin were by no means universally accepted in their time; their music sounded strange and dissonant to a lot of people. So these critics posited that maybe we just needed the same adjustment process for atonal music and its spin-offs.

Of course this level of popularity has never come to pass and yet the original works of atonal music, serial music, and other innovations are now many decades old. Schoenberg's *Pierrot Lunaire* song cycle premiered in 1912—almost one hundred years ago—and I don't know anyone who holds out hope for its eventual cultural ascendancy.

If anything, many strands of contemporary music have become less listenable over time to the majority of music listeners. I know listeners who appreciate Schoenberg and Berg, or perhaps Messiaen, but they draw the line at Carter, Boulez, Babbitt, and Stockhausen, not to mention Helmut Lachenmann or James Tenney or David Tudor (some of my favorites). Sometimes these composers don't produce much more than what—to others—would seem like a loud, screeching tone.

It's not that the skeptics are indifferent to this music. Many people hate this music, or they would hate it if they had to hear it more often. They don't hate it for cultural reasons, as some northeastern elites dislike county-and-western styles for their broader "red state" connotations, but rather they hate it because of the way it sounds. They hate how it hurts their ears and violates their aesthetic sensibilities. They hate its ugliness. The music comes across—to many people—as scratchy, disconnected, and moving from one obnoxious noise to another. Yet that's exactly the same music that I sometimes use to relax if I've just had a strenuous time making small talk at a cocktail party.

Neither sociology nor aesthetic argument will solve this one, but maybe neurology will. I think of a lot of atonal music as music for the neurodiverse, and again I mean that word in the broad sense. Just as many people hate the sound of the music, there is no denying that many serious listeners—albeit a definite minority—find it compelling.

Why exactly might some people prefer atonal music and similar forms? One possibility is that many individuals use different methods of organizing sounds in a hierarchy and this leads them to prefer different musical and indeed sonic content. For instance if the perception of sound is more immediate and less regulated by top-down processes, some pure sounds will be hated and others will be enjoyed, depending on the details of neurology. Many autistics have strong dislikes of sirens, beeping sounds, the confusion of multiple voices, and "normal" levels of background noise. Other individuals (some of whom are autistic, but not mostly) have *preferred* sounds, as reflected in the diverse offerings available in music markets. A lot of twentieth- and twenty-first-century classical music, starting with Varese and John Cage, blurs the distinction between music and the more general notion of sound; those musics appeal to subgroups that have special sonic likes and dislikes. One practical lesson is that "music as noise" is an entirely coherent aesthetic phenomenon, whether you find it in the contemporary classical composers or in a modern "noise band" such as Merzbow.

The studies of atonal music in the music cognition literature show that most people have trouble putting the music in a meaningful hierarchy. Atonal music tends to have less structure at the larger scales of sonic organization—at least in terms of orders that most people can enjoy—and so to unappreciative listeners it sounds like random noise. You won't find traditional harmonies or hummable tunes. With additional listening to a piece, repeated motifs often become apparent, but they're hard to find and they don't satisfy most people in the way that the progressive elucidation of a Haydn motif does, much less a Buddy Holly song. So understanding or appreciating the structure of atonal music requires some special skills of pattern recognition. The atonal music fans may be better at some kinds of cognitive processing, and better at constructing some kinds of hierarchies from their sensory input, relative to typical listeners.

When viewed through this lens of neurology, many of the critical dialogues about contemporary music seem beside the point, as they don't get at the real source of the difference of opinion. Diana Raffman, a philosopher at the University of Toronto, wrote an essay that surveys the cognitive difficulties behind appreciating atonal music and she concludes that it, as music, must not be an acceptable art form. The remarkable things about this essay are that she a) never considers neurodiversity across human beings, and b) never comes to terms with the fact that this music has some real fans. My working hypothesis is that, to put it bluntly, most of humanity has a cognitive disability when it comes to enjoying atonal music.

Part of the joy in atonal music and related forms is discovering the order and in the meantime enjoying the surprise of what is to come next. In atonal music the order is harder to find than usual and thus perhaps the music has an appeal a bit like that of solving a difficult crossword puzzle or breaking a cipher. But for that to be fun you have to face some prospect of actually breaking the code, albeit not too easily.

The idea of finding order in music may sound mechanical but it shouldn't be so unfamiliar. Many people like to think of themselves as preferring emotion in music and not structure or order, but these qualities are closely connected. For most of us, finding the order in the music should be neither too easy nor too hard. That's why we don't listen to simple pop ditties too many times in a row; after a while the tune becomes expected and it no longer stimulates us in a pleasing manner or gives us enough emotion. In other words, the music doesn't have a complex enough structure for most of us and hearing it is like doing a crossword puzzle we already have solved. It's why tic-tac-toe isn't a fun game for most of us.

An issue arises if you get "too good" at finding the order in music. You must resort to bigger and bigger doses of informational complexity to achieve the prior effects that were so enjoyable. It's a bit like needing successively stronger doses of heroin, wanting to move beyond Vivaldi, or more prosaically having to switch from one pop song to the next. Don't we all do that? But the metric for the right amount of complexity differs across listeners, even across listeners with the same degree of musical experience and education.

The kid who listens only to Top 40 might feel that your love for Mahler is overly intellectualized, when for you Mahler is joy and pathos. I swooned over the Beethoven symphonies as a youth but today that's not enough for me. I get a visceral and electrifying surge from, say, a live performance by the Master Musicians of Jajouka, a microtonal noise band from rural Morocco that probably would hurt your ears. Live Indian classical music, especially of the percussive variety (Zakir Hussain is a special favorite) is for me also an emotionally ecstatic experience. Indian classical music, which does not rely so heavily on all-too-predictable harmonies, produces for me more excitement and raw emotion. Some people may need a more violent "feel" to their music, just as Kiriana Cowansage likes pictures and stories with lots of contrast and sharp relief. Atonal music, with its lack of traditional harmony and melody, often sounds brutal and discordant, as does the noise band from Morocco, and that is part of what I like about it.

I was curious and I asked Kiriana Cowansage what role music played in her life. Her answer, as you might expect, reflects the diversity of individual taste:

> I listen to music—usually only one or two songs on repeat for a month or more. Then I spontaneously get bored and switch. Usually, for about a week after such a switch, the new song makes me feel loopy and euphoric—I can't focus on any other activity—so I have to break in new songs for a period of time before I can use them as background. I have a similar reaction (face heating up, euphoria) to certain fast-paced rhythms and parts that crescendo or mount. In orchestral music, I like dark and rhythmic pieces, for example, Dance of the Knights. Despite this, I've never developed a real interest in music, beyond the listening part. I don't follow any particular artists and I don't have a favorite. In fact, I often can't name the song that I've been listening to for a month. I seem to latch onto internal

elements of a song without caring about it as a whole or the artist in general.

A lot of what we don't like, in the arts, is simply creative forms that appeal to different and perhaps unusual neurologies. I am not saying that all people with unusual neurologies love atonal music or for that matter even know much about atonal music. It's just that if I go to a concert of contemporary classical music—the scratchy kind—I expect to see people with rather specialized cognitive skills, including the ability to order sounds that can easily seem chaotic into a comprehensible hierarchy.

Atonal and serialist music represent further signs of the division of productive labor present in all economically advanced societies. The world has become so wealthy and so diverse that some composers make music that appeals to people only with a very particular and very refine sense of musical appreciation. That's the best way to think about much of the music—and other art forms—that you may hate.

As with atonal music, the most common reaction is simply to evaluate the aesthetic perspective through the taste of either the public or the educated critics. We privilege those perspectives either because they have social status or because, in the case of the consumers, they have buying power and thus they command the attention of the media. So if it is serial killer stories, maybe the critics call it too lowbrow and talk about the decline of our society. If it is atonal music, it gets labeled as too inaccessible or too highbrow or it is claimed that the academic composers are perverse and self-indulgent. Most cultural criticism is staggering in how much it begs the question of what is the appropriate middle ground.

In the meantime, awareness of human neurodiversity helps us see the diversity of beauty in modern society, even if we cannot perceive all of those beauties. As cultural production becomes more diverse, more and more art forms will be directed at pleasing people with unusual neurologies. More and more of the aesthetic beauty of the world will be hidden to most observers, or at least those who don't invest in learning. The aesthetic lushness of the world will be increasingly distributed into baroque nooks and crannies, in a manner that would honor a Borges short story.

It's not usually put in such terms, but I think of *art connoisseurship* as a fundamental part of the profile of autistics. Go back to the list of the cognitive strengths of autism in chapter 2. Autistics have, on average, superior visual perception, a better-developed sense of pitch, superior abilities for pattern recognition, and superior abilities for spotting details in visual pictures, compared to non-autistics. Yet, as discussed in chapter 6, autistics may be less skilled at enjoying some kinds of fictional narrative.

Dr. Hans Asperger saw the aesthetic side of autistics clearly. He wrote:

> Another distinctive trait one finds in some autistic children is a rare maturity of taste in art. Normal children have no time for more sophisticated art. Their taste is usually for the pretty picture, with kitschy rose pink and sky blue . . . Autistic children, on the other hand, can have a surprisingly sophisticated understanding, being able to distinguish between art and kitsch with great confidence. They may have a special understanding of works of art which are difficult even for many adults, for

instance Romanesque sculpture or paintings by Rembrandt. Autistic individuals can judge accurately the events represented in the picture, as well as what lies behind them, including the character of the people represented and the mood that pervades a painting. Consider that many normal adults never reach this mature degree of art appreciation.

As I discussed in chapter 5, autistics often do not need cultural canons to appreciate aesthetic qualities in objects or artworks. Remember Sue Rubin and her appreciation for plastic spoons and running water? Hugo Lamoureux, a Canadian autistic, reports that watching the snow removal equipment in Quebec is for him a highly enjoyable endeavor. There is no full or satisfactory account of what autistics are doing when they focus on favored objects in such a manner. But in part autistics seem to be appreciating some aesthetic qualities of these objects, without the intermediation of what non-autistics would normally call works of art. The autistics are cutting through to the underlying beauties of form, color, texture, and so on without requiring a mainstream, socially constructed context in between themselves and those qualities of interest. These autistics live in a joyous and plentiful artistic world, but because their enjoyment relies less on social intermediation and formal canons of taste and interpretation, that enjoyment is harder for others to perceive.

The gap here is not a simple one of "autistics vs. non-autistics." Remember there is a great deal of variety of perceptual skills across autistics. For that reason, if no other, each autistic is likely to focus on varying objects for his or her aesthetic preferences. The preferences of one autistic will not necessarily be intelligible, in specific terms, to the understanding of another autistic. For that reason there is not an "autistic cultural canon" to stand alongside the non-autistic cultural canons. The lack of such a canon may look like a weakness but it also can be viewed as a strength: Aesthetic appreciation through the lens of a canon is optional for autistics. Maybe a cultural canon is a kind of perceptual crutch, or a device for framing, which many autistics simply don't need. As I've mentioned, the autistics are in this regard closer to some ideas in Buddhism; they can see the beauty of the universe in very small or very particular objects.

You may recall Arthur Danto's famous essay on why Andy Warhol's Brillo box is art when a normal Brillo box, before Warhol, was never considered art. The box is more or less the same. Danto's answer, in a nutshell, was that art must be defined in an appropriate social context and historical understanding. The earlier Brillo box—before Warhol—lacked this complementary understanding. But Danto is never clear on how large a social "art world" is needed to create this context. Do we need a large nation? A midsized nation? A small group of art critics? What if Warhol's Brillo boxes are understood as art only in Iceland, population 300,000 or so? What if the relevant understanding is held in the mind of only a single individual? You can see where this is headed: Create your own economy.

If autistics have greater direct and independent access to the aesthetic qualities of objects, they are less reliant on the traditional artistic paths toward accessing beauty and wonder. It seems that for many autistics art is more powerful but also more optional at the same time. That's an unusual and indeed, for many of us, counterintuitive combination.

That said, this counterintuitive combination should be increasingly familiar to us, albeit through a different mode of access, namely technology rather than cognition rooted in neurology. Recall from chapter 3 that many of us, through web technology, are replacing traditional artistic masterworks with our personal blends of self-assembled small cultural bits. The iPhone and its outputs have surpassed the classic masterworks as a representation of where culture is at today. Masterworks, such as Caravaggio paintings, are more accessible than ever before and it is easier to learn about them and learn to love them too. That makes masterworks more powerful, at least for those who care. At the same time, not everyone needs Caravaggio. If you don't look at his paintings, or if you don't experience other classic parts of the Western canon, your self-assembled aesthetic life still can be a rich one. For most of us it can be said that art is now becoming more powerful but also more optional at the same time.

And that makes the world more beautiful.

9

AUTISTIC POLITICS

World politics so often seems gloomy. Wars are bloody and frequent, most nations have high levels of corruption and lots of bad governance, and, even in the most successful polities, bitter partisanship prevents many important problems from being solved in a forward-looking manner. You probably agree with this short portrait, no matter what the details of your political stance.

Those outcomes are not inevitable but to see improvement we need to overcome some of our cognitive biases. That's right, a lot of the problems of politics stem from human cognition. It's not always a question of strengthening "the good guys" who are fighting "the bad guys." We all tend to think we are the good guys more often than we really are. We fight when we should give in, we stick to our guns when we should change our mind, and we do not realize that we are sometimes part of the problem rather than the solution. If we are to improve politics, we need to help ourselves overcome these biases.

My colleague Robin Hanson runs a website called Overcoming Bias (www.overcomingbias.com) and that phrase reflects a central theme in his thought: How biased are we humans and what can we do to overcome those biases? I've long been a fan of Robin's efforts to clear the world of false thinking and toward that end he is fascinated with cognitive biases, emotional biases, biases from overestimating our own abilities, and so on. Robin also attaches special importance to our bias to think we are smarter than are other people. We tend to attach more weight to our own opinions, when those opinions clash with equally smart others, than is rationally justifiable. How many people do you know who walk away from half their arguments saying that the other guy was right?

One way to correct for those biases is to check in with the perspectives of other people. And so I wonder: If we can learn something from autistic perspectives on aesthetics, what might we learn from autistic perspectives on politics? How could that contribute to self-education and the creation of my own economy? But of course we must first ask what it means to postulate an autistic perspective on politics. Autistics are not themselves associated with any particular political point of view, except perhaps for better treatment of autistics. If autism is fundamentally a cognitive profile, how can that possibly be mapped into the complex, messy world of real-world politics?

I believe that autistics are especially well equipped to appreciate modes of political thinking that are cosmopolitan and legalistic (in the sense of favoring rule of law), and more broadly the notion of a pragmatic "politics without romance." I would like to offer some admittedly speculative perspectives on these questions.

I start with a simple but little-known observation: There is good evidence that people along the autism spectrum are in some measurable ways more objective than non-autistics. It remains an open question how far this objectivity extends, but, from psychologist Rita R. Jordan, here is a typical description of the current scientific consensus:

People with ASD [autism spectrum disorder] are therefore less likely to show egocentric, or other, bias. They are also protected from bias by the failure of their memories to adjust to existing context or to their general semantic knowledge. Thinking (including remembering) is unusually objective in people with ASDs . . . and memories remain both rigid and accurate (in relation to the time of their encoding). Such detailed discrimination of the particular should mean that people with autism are not prone to stereotyping in their thinking or memories.

We should not conclude that autistics are more objective about everything (we just don't know), but the difference in perspective is intriguing.

Another well-known bias, familiar from behavioral economics, is called the endowment effect. People tend to place excess value on the objects they already own or perceive as belonging to them.

Some recent research ("Explaining Enhanced Logical Consistency During Decision Making in Autism" by Benedetto De Martino et al.) suggests autistics are less likely to suffer from endowment effects and in this regard they are more likely to behave according to standards of economic rationality. A classic laboratory experiment starts people with a sum of money, in this case fifty British pounds, and offers them a comparison between two sure options: "keeping twenty pounds" and "losing thirty pounds." Given the starting point of fifty pounds, the two actual outcomes are the same, even though one framing sounds positive and the other framing sounds negative. But will people treat them the same? In the experiment the subjects are asked to compare the two sure outcomes to a series of risks. The economically correct answer is to view the two sure outcomes as equal in comparing them to the series of risks. But in the laboratory subjects typically are more averse to the prospect framed in terms of a loss ("loss aversion"). More specifically, once the outcome is framed in terms of a loss, people will accept greater gambles to try to avoid any loss at all, compared to the risks they will take when the position is framed in terms of gains.

In the study, the autistic subjects did significantly better at seeing that the talk of "loss" and "gain" was mere framing and that the two options should be treated the same, although they too showed some degree of loss aversion. Skin conductance tests run during the experiment indicated that the autistics reacted less emotionally to framing the one option in terms of loss rather than gain. In other words, the mere fact that a material resource is viewed as "theirs" seems to bias autistics less than it does non-autistics.

I'll come back to those results, but first let's look at some autistic perspectives on politics.

I have noticed that self-aware autistics are especially likely to be cosmopolitans in their thinking. That is, they tend to attach weaker moral importance to the boundaries of the nation state than do most other people. I view the relative lack of cosmopolitan sympathies as a bias held by others and a case where the autistic perception, if I may call it that, is closer to being the correct one. Since war has been very

costly in human history, I view the benefits of the less biased cosmopolitan perspective as significant.

Much of this cosmopolitan tendency is rooted in experience
rather than cognition. Most autistics have lots of experience with
being the "out group" when it comes to "in vs. out" confrontations or
social settings. That makes them naturally suspicious of political per-
secutions, extreme forms of patriotism, and groupthink. Autistics are
in any case less synchronized with mainstream social fads, as we
have seen.

In 2008, a Florida classroom voted 14–2 to expel a five-year-old
boy labeled as Asperger's. The teacher held an impromptu "trial" of
the boy, in front of the class, with testimony from his five-year-old
detractors. Each student was asked to say something he or she did
not like about the boy and many called him "weird" or put forward
related epithets. Then the vote was held, again at the instigation of
the teacher. (I am heartened by the two votes to keep the boy in class
and I would have liked to have heard an exit poll from his defenders.)
This is an extreme example, and the teacher was later removed from
that post, but it represents an all-too-familiar tendency to pick on
people who are different and unable to defend themselves.

So to the extent nationalism is based on cultivating or encouraging an "in group" feeling, it probably won't appeal much to autistics.
Many autistics will be wary of nationalism and they will see it as
rooted in the same in-group feelings that led to their taunting or oppression in the schoolyard or elsewhere.

To a self-aware autistic, nations, or for that matter religions, will
not always seem like the most important moral dividing lines. The

general phenomenon of neurodiversity implies that within a single nation or religion individuals can be very different. Two autistic individuals in Baltimore and Beijing might have some important features of cognition or behavior in common and they might feel stronger bonds with each other than either would with many of their countrymen.

The association of diversity with national boundaries or with regional geography is built into a great deal of the contemporary discussion of globalization, both among scholars and in the popular arena. If the nation of France becomes more like the nation of Germany, there is a presumption that "cultural diversity" has gone down. When people in Bangkok started wearing blue jeans and thus neglected native modes of dress, a wide array of commentators, from Naomi Klein to Benjamin Barber, suggest that such instances show a decline in cultural diversity. These writers asked how much one geographical region differs from another, and using that benchmark, they judged the progress of cultural diversity.

But why should we focus on the form of diversity that lines up so closely with physical space, national boundaries, and "face time"?

Many of the most important forms of human diversity, including neurodiversity, don't line up with geography in any simple way. Self-aware autistic individuals are more likely to be aware of the diversity across people's minds, neurologies, and behavior patterns. When I know that autistics are using the web to organize, to teach each other about social interaction, and to make new friends I think: "Ah, diversity is going up!" Of course these trends go far beyond autistics and they cover newly organized groups of many different kinds. Suddenly there is greater space and latitude for many pursuits, experiences, and ways of life. Only later do I wonder whether these people are in separate countries or in the same country or whether their countries are becoming more alike. It's a bias to focus so heavily on one's countrymen, or any other form of in-group relations.

There also may be more fundamental cognitive reasons for an autistic predisposition toward cosmopolitan attitudes. A nation or culture is a bit like an endowment effect, namely that most people value it more highly, with special degrees of fervor, simply because it is theirs. Herodotus remarked long ago that each person thinks that his way of life is best. You can find exceptions, but if you look, say, at the wars in the former Yugoslavia, most Serbs favored the Serbian side, most Bosnians favored the Bosnian side, and so on. There were Soviet dissidents who hoped their country would be conquered by the United States but overall political "turncoats" of this kind are relatively rare. Most people take the side of their country or their culture or their region, simply because it is theirs.

If autistics suffer less from the bias of endowment effects, perhaps they are also less likely to value a nation highly, again, simply because it is theirs. Autistics may be more able to take an objective point of view. I again stress that this is speculative, but it is a first step toward contemplating autistic perspectives on politics.

When it comes to political theory, my expectation is twofold. First, autistics are attracted to simple and straightforward codes of ethics, applied universally to all human beings. Apart from autistic cosmopolitanism and autistic objectivity, it also may stem from a greater willingness to question whether socially common exceptions to the rules are justified.

Second, I suspect that a subgroup of autistics has a relatively easy time accepting or grasping ideas about constitutions, rules-based approaches to social order, legal reasoning as it is written down, and the long-term impersonal benefits of the rule of law. Appreciating the abstract operation of any mechanism, whether a watch, a machine, an economy, or a polity (or atonal music; see the previous chapter), is quite difficult. We should expect to find that skill in relative or disproportionate surplus among groups that have a comparative advantage in understanding ordered, abstract mechanisms. Appreciating the practical benefits of a free society—at a high level of abstraction—may be correlated (loosely) with autism in the same way that math or engineering or clock repair skills are. Some small subgroup of autistics is especially likely to have those skills, even if autistics as a whole usually do not.

Again, the claim is not that autistics are "more this way on average." Instead cognitive specialization and varied cognitive skills will put autistics into various intellectual nooks and crannies, in a wide variety of directions, political or otherwise.

Writing the Declaration of Independence surely required an extraordinary ability to look afresh at an important problem. There is in fact a heated debate as to whether or not Thomas Jefferson was on the autism spectrum, in part due to his extreme propensity to collect and catalog information. As I have discussed, the difficulties of any diagnosis across history are daunting and I don't think it is possible to categorize Jefferson in this manner. The point stands that unusual or important ideas—just like unusual aesthetic perspectives—often come from people with specialized cognitive skills. Living in 2009, we often take ideas about a free society for granted but in fact such ideas have been totally absent throughout most of human history and they still have not taken hold in many parts of our world. An understanding of a free society and its benefits does not come naturally to most human beings and that understanding had to be discovered and communicated by people with some highly atypical minds.

On average autistics are better with print-based modes of reasoning than with oral discourse. Many autistics have a strong memory for factual details, strong pattern recognition skills, and an ability to interpret principles of equality very literally and in a cosmopolitan manner. These are exactly the sorts of skills that go into legalistic and constitutional reasoning. Furthermore those skills are especially relevant in appreciating social systems based on written laws, rather than systems based on unspoken or implicit personal favors.

One thinker who did very much appreciate the abstract workings of the economy—and a good legal system—was the late economics Nobel laureate Friedrich A. Hayek (though I would not suggest Hayek was autistic). Hayek stressed that the market economy was an effective abstract mechanism for coordinating plans and discovering new ideas; he also favored a constitutional order based on the rule of law and equal treatment for all human beings. In his *Constitution of Liberty* and other works, Hayek outlined a vision of a liberal society as a "spontaneous order," namely a proliferation of institutions, conventions, norms, and other social and economic practices that are not generally the result of central planning. Most of all Hayek is skeptical about the ability of human beings to plan all outcomes in advance by using their reason. Hayek argued that a rich and largely unplanned order can blossom when society is governed by a relatively small set of abstract rules, and, ideally, a constitution; you don't have to share Hayek's libertarian and conservative version of this blend to find this an appealing vision.

Hayek also thought his political arguments should be grounded in an understanding of human neurology. Before the Second World War he wrote a work that was later titled *The Sensory Order* (the book was not published until 1952). This book, a study in neurology, reflects many of the broader themes of knowledge and interpretation in Hayek's work. Hayek argues that the mind is governed by the decentralized classification of sensory inputs. Cognition is not about top-down processes or a unitary decision-maker sitting in a single mental chair. In Hayek's view the spontaneous mental order, resulting from the ongoing classification of sensory inputs, makes cognition possible while limiting the ability of our mind to know reality in all its fullness. In an argument reminiscent of Gödel, Hayek stresses how a decentralized process of classification can never fully understand itself and thus can never fully understand the social world. Hayek was one of the first neuroeconomists (probably Adam Smith was the first), and while he showed no interest in autism, his core model of the mind touches on some key issues of autistic cognition.

Hayek's neurological analysis isn't informed by recent scientific research but it is nonetheless significant that he takes neurology to be so important for his projects in economics and political philosophy. If the imperfections of human knowledge drive Hayek's arguments on politics and economics, the natural inclination is to want to understand knowledge better and thus he was led to study neurology.

My perspective on politics and neurology is, however, a bit different from Hayek's. He tries to argue something like "A mind cannot very well understand itself and so a polity cannot reshape itself effectively according to principles of rational argument." That leads Hayek to some relatively conservative conclusions, along the lines of the classic British conservative Edmund Burke. Hayek repeatedly stresses the dangers of revising long-standing institutions all at once according to some supposedly rational plan; he fears that the limits of the human mind will cause such plans to overreach and go askew. I don't see a strong correlation between how well a mind can know itself and how well a government can make broader plans for society. Hayek's work on neurology, even if correct on its own terms, did not succeed in justifying or grounding his political ideas.

My core intuition is more along these lines: "Different kinds of human minds often have difficulty appreciating each other's virtues, so social arrangements, and personal individual judgments, should be robust to this fact." That is still an argument for social and economic decentralization, but it has a different slant than Hayek's. In most disputes, cosmopolitan perspectives that include an appreciation of abstract social hierarchies are likely to be undervalued by most people and they shouldn't be. As is probably obvious by now, I think autistic perspectives on politics are extremely valuable.

Autistic insights won't, on their own, settle the debates between Democrats and Republicans or between libertarians and progressives or whatever the dispute may be. But when combined with other values and empirical judgments, those principles will influence our political conclusions. Those principles could make us less partisan, more willing to cooperate, more willing to admit we cannot judge every issue correctly, and, most importantly, less willing to define politics in terms of "us vs. them." Such changes would improve the political problems discussed in the first paragraph of this chapter, namely war, corruption, and bad governance.

Consider the eighteenth-century German philosopher Immanuel

Kant. (Warning: Two paragraphs of abstruse metaphysics will follow; skip them if you wish!) If there is any thinker who exhibited a very general attraction to the ideas of rules and ordering, whether in personal or public life, it is Kant. Perhaps more than any other thinker of his time, Kant stressed the importance of how the mind orders reality (Kant, by the way, influenced Hayek). For Kant this was not neurology but rather it was a fundamental metaphysical principle. He was trying to solve the debates of his time about how human beings can possibly know anything at all. He doubted the constructions of the rationalists, who claimed to deduce knowledge from pure reasoning alone; he thought pure reason taken alone would collapse in contradictions and dead ends. He also was unpersuaded by the empiricists, such as John Locke and David Hume, who looked to sensations in the mind as a source of knowledge. Kant did not see how the mere accumulation of particular pieces of knowledge about our sensations could possibly lead to something as powerful and as certain as mathematics and geometry. In essence Kant set out to refute skepticism about the possibility of knowledge, and he did this by emphasizing how our minds order reality and thus make possible knowledge of that reality.

With this talk of order and ordering, Kant wasn't referring to daily acts of classification and collection but rather that our minds contribute rational underlying structures to the entire universe, including the categories of space and time. Order comes from our ordering processes. For Kant, we know reality not because our minds perceive it passively but because we help create it. Furthermore we can never know things in themselves ("noumena") but rather we have access only to how our minds impose structure on things. Much of

Kant's *Critique of Pure Reason* outlined his account of the categories and rules that the mind contributes to reality in this "synthetic" fashion. In Kant's terminology of "phenomena" and "noumena," we can never know noumena but we know phenomena by helping to create them with our minds.

Maybe that sounds a little heady and if you don't understand it all, I'm not sure that I do either. In fact I'm not sure that, if you look at it closely enough, it makes much sense. Metaphysics slips easily into ill-defined concepts and without clarity of language metaphysical ideas can be very hard to understand, much less evaluate. But still, Kant was obsessed with the idea—no matter how exactly you interpret it—that the mind orders reality.

Kant's biography shows that ordering took on many forms in his life, not just in his epistemology and metaphysics. Kant ordered his own reality through his regular walks, through his interest in mastering human knowledge, and through his attempt to construct a failsafe philosophical system. Ordering was such a strong idea and also practice for Kant that when it came to metaphysics, apparently it was natural that ordering should assume primary place. I read Kant as, quite simply, a brilliant but biased thinker who elevated neurology to the realm of metaphysics. Kantian metaphysics is a kind of autistic dream, as if the specialized cognitive strengths of the autistic mind somehow were fundamental to all of reality.

In Kant's life the idea of ordering pops up in many different contexts. Kant was a polymath and he devoted his life to accumulating and organizing knowledge. He taught a wide variety of courses, including mathematics, geography, anthropology, the natural sciences, metaphysics, logic, theology, ethics, and pedagogy, and he was renowned for having expertise in all of these areas. Kant never married or seemed to have an active sex life. He actively socialized but usually toward the end of intellectual conversation and engagement. It is reputed that the citizens of Königsberg, where Kant lived, set their clocks by his daily walk. It's hard to tell how much of those historical accounts is exaggeration, but it is known that Kant lived a quiet academic life and avoided small changes in his daily routines. His letters show that noise and noisy environments disturbed him greatly. We don't know if Kant was autistic but the idea of ordering—now in the sense of overt behavior rather than cognition—had a strong hold over his life.

If you look at Kant's ethical and political ideas, they reflect his fascination with ordering. He favored a very strict morality of obligation based on the idea of fixed rules of conduct that were not to be broken under any circumstances. We should not for instance tell lies, even to save human lives. In the more practical political sphere, Kant was a strong and early advocate of the rule of law, constitutionalism, and political liberty, including a cosmopolitan world order of peace. Kant had a strong appreciation for the operation of abstract mechanisms.

What has gone wrong with many of the non-free societies in today's world is a lack of adherence to abstract rules of behavior and a lack of understanding of such rules as beneficial abstract mechanisms. A country where people do not wait in line in orderly fashion, or where the drivers do not stay in their lanes, is usually a country with serious economic and political problems. It is instructive to compare rule-following behavior in Chile and Argentina. In Chile people are far more likely to obey the laws and to obey the unspoken rules, and they make these decisions of their own accord without the prospect of immediate reward or punishment. You cannot bribe a policeman and most drivers follow the rules of the road. Overall the country is remarkably non-corrupt, especially compared to its neighbors, including Argentina. Chile is also more prosperous than Argentina and for some time now its political life has been more stable and also freer. Contemporary Chile is by most accounts the most successful society in Latin America. In most Latin American countries—but not Chile—the system of income tax collection does not function. You can argue about whether rule-following behavior is the cause or effect of the Chilean success but probably it is both.

A list of the most successful societies in the world usually would include the United Kingdom, the Nordic countries, Japan, the United States, Canada, Australia, and New Zealand. Rule-governed behavior is a paramount idea and indeed ideal in each of these societies. The Hungarian émigré George Mikes noticed that "an Englishman, even if he is alone, forms an orderly queue of one."

For an example of political failure, consider contemporary Russia. Despite a substantial freeing up of the economy after the fall of the Soviet Union and a well-educated population, Russia today is not a free society. It does not have free speech, most of the resources are state-controlled or mafia-controlled monopolies, and corruption is rampant. Democracy is vanishing as each election is more controlled than the last. Freedom of the press is dwindling.

Many Russians value freedom but their conception of freedom is not tied to a comparable understanding of the benefits of rules or how rules can operate as a useful abstract mechanism. Too many Russians lack a strong idea of adherence to the norms and principles behind a free society. Instead most Russians, including most of the numerous freedom-loving ones, find their first attachment to their friends and to an ideal of friendship. Their attachments are highly emotional and directed toward very particular human connections, not toward the abstract or toward a principle of order. The connection to friends also comes before the duty to country or the idea of loyalty to an abstract principle of order.

Many Russians are cynical about large-scale political units and for that matter about large-scale political principles. And because of both the Great War and communism, they are used to relying on friends to survive. So in any political setting the natural tendency is toward particularism, favoritism, and that means corruption too. General civic spirit is weak and written constitutions have little or no meaning. Political life degenerates into a grab for resources and few people stop or protest on the grounds that this is breaking some set of explicit or implicit rules. And so we are seeing a descent into tyranny and control once again. Yet at the same time most Russians are incredibly warm and loving human beings (I don't just say that because I married one . . .). That warmth reflects their deep and very personal ties to their circles of friends and families.

But where is the attachment to an ideal of abstract order in the political sphere? The notion of abstract orders is found in many areas of Russian life—just look at all the phenomenal Russian chess players—but sadly it is not much found in the Russian conception of the polity.

As I write, Russia is losing the potential to become a free society.

And why? We've already seen that autistics have cognitive strengths at mental ordering, and also that many autistics have cognitive advantages in understanding the benefits of abstractly ordered systems. It can be said that the overall Russian mind-set, when it comes to politics, is not sufficiently autistic.

10

THE FUTURE OF THE UNIVERSE

Why not get a little audacious? We've seen how mainstream society is reaping benefits from mimicking autistic cognitive strengths. We have become more passionate about information. We have become more adept at manipulating small bits of information and weaving those small bits into an emotionally satisfying narrative, even if the suspense and beauty of that narrative is not always visible to outsiders. We're getting much better at entertaining ourselves and also at educating ourselves. As our inner lives become richer, the idea of creating your own economy is becoming a reality. We're learning how to use filters to get the information we really want and we are learning how to avoid information overload. We're learning how to cultivate intellectual patience. And every day we are getting better at using the web to connect with other human beings and improve our personal relationships. Most of all, by mimicking some traits of autistics, we are becoming more human. What's next?

We could benefit in further ways by adopting a better and deeper understanding of human neurodiversity. We could have a more practical understanding of the limits of formal education. We could be more skeptical about story-based reasoning and superficially appealing narratives; we also could become more resistant to obnoxious advertising and less bent on senseless revenge. We could understand better how a different mind can be an entertaining mind and perhaps also a heroic mind. We could treat minorities, including autistic people, better. We could appreciate new and different forms of music and art, or at least we could be more tolerant of diverging aesthetic tastes. We could become better citizens, more cosmopolitan, more objective about our culture and nation, and better able to appreciate the benefits of the rule of law.

That's for society as a whole. But I'd like to consider one of its parts: What about people who are themselves autistic? They may well reap some of the improvements mentioned above but how are their fortunes evolving in modern society more generally?

Autistics face many problems and obstacles, but overall I am optimistic. Most of all, many autistics are benefiting from the web. In particular the web allows people to exchange ideas without being in each other's physical presence. Since many autistics find public circulation to be exhausting (to varying degrees), this is for them an enormous benefit. Autistics can exchange ideas and feelings with other people—including of course other autistics—with greater ease than before. It's not just email and websites. There are multiple forums in Second Life, the online virtual reality platform, where autistics IM and talk to each other, build virtual museums to neurodiversity and its heroes, and exchange tips on how to handle social interactions with non-autistics. That was not possible ten years ago.

It's not hard to imagine further advances through new technologies. For instance the many autistics who do not speak intelligibly, yet who are highly intelligent, could use iPhones or related devices to communicate to others in public. The iPhone already can take queries and give answers through voice recognition software; a modification could allow the typing of an autistic person to be converted into intelligible speech.

Autistics are using the web to augment their cognitive strengths. Let's say that an autistic person is relatively good at rapidly absorbing new blocks of information, analyzing that information, and interpreting, ordering, and repackaging the result in written form. The web gives autistics a medium in which those strengths are amplified and then broadcast to large numbers of other people. Autistic cognitive skills are more likely to rise to a status when they are admired, even though those skills are rarely recognized as such. Overall there are many media for mental ordering on the web and autistics have a comparative advantage at working with these media and indeed inventing them. Tony Attwood, a well-known autism and Asperger's clinician, has noted that when he gives a public talk he can fill a normal-sized room; when he gives a public talk in Silicon Valley six hundred people will show up. There are some good reasons for the stereotypical association of autistics with information technology.

The web has elevated the primacy of the written word in our culture. This benefits the numerous autistics who are more skilled in written communication than in face-to-face verbal communication. The move of so much economic and cultural activity to the web makes these autistic lives much easier.

For autistics it's a stroke of luck that the written word and the image have been so elevated by recent technology. Olaf Stapledon, the early British science writer, postulated in his 1937 novel *Star*

Maker a technological revolution that would beam touch, taste, smell, and sound into our lives: "In civilized countries everyone but the pariahs carried a pocket receiving set . . . The place of music was taken by taste- and smell-themes, which were translated into patterns of ethereal undulation, transmitted by all the great national stations, and restored to their original form in the pocket receivers and taste-batteries of the population. These instruments afforded intricate stimuli to the taste organs and scent organs of the hand." "Sexual" broadcasting is sent to the brain directly. In general, "radio-brain-stimulation" became the most important avocation in this society.

Maybe that sounds like fun to you (maybe not), but Stapledon's postulated technological revolution would be less fun for many autistic people, especially those who are easily overwhelmed by additional sounds, smells, and tastes. Instead we have received a visually oriented technological revolution—this time at least—and to the benefit of many autistics.

We are witnessing the first generation of autistic, Asperger's, and neurodiverse people to grow up with an explicit (if only partial) understanding of their neurologies and an ability to communicate with each other en masse. This will hardly eliminate all of the problems of autistics. But still, this development is unprecedented in world history and I expect it to increase the happiness and productivity of autistic people. I also hope that this book can, in some small way, contribute to this overall trend.

On a national scale, the United States is doing relatively well in mobilizing its autistic talents. The American culture of nonconformity, geographic mobility, lots of empty space, and tolerance of outsiders is in some regards relatively well suited for autistics. Youth is respected and the personal contacts that come with seniority are not always required to get a good job, at least not compared to most other parts of the world.

High-tech and higher education, long-standing American success stories, have created natural homes for many productive autistics. Since it seems these sectors will continue to grow and that American nonconformism will flourish, autistics will be able to find more niches. Of course the whole world benefits from mobilizing autistic talent, since high-tech ideas spread globally and, when it comes to the academic world, students from around the world come to study in the United States. No one planned it this way, but America has created a very special environment for nurturing the creativity of diverse talents.

Many of the new and positive trends remind me of the reasoning behind classical economics. You may know that the division of labor is a key idea in Adam Smith's *Wealth of Nations*. Smith's notion of the division of labor referred to increasing specialization in economic production. He gives the example, from a pin factory, of how each worker performs a very specific and repetitive task in the interests of greater productivity for the factory as a whole.

It's not what Smith intended, but I read this discussion of the pin factory as a parable of autism and the rising returns to autistic cognitive strengths. If you can perform a repetitive task with the proper skill, you can earn a decent income because you are no longer expected to be a jack-of-all-trades or to master a wide variety of skills. It increases the chance that you can have a "dysfunction" and still do well in life and in your career. We don't all have to feed the chickens in the morning, plow the fields in the afternoon, and repair our shoes in the evening. We don't have to court the village elites and be socially well connected. Today it's often enough to be very good at one specific professional task. In other words, the division of labor provides disproportionate benefits to people with specialized cognitive talents and that includes many people along the autism spectrum. It's yet another way in which modernity supports diversity.

Smith, like Karl Marx later on, feared that the division of labor would be boring and alienating in its specialized and repetitive tasks. For many people, however, the resulting ability to specialize is more of a benefit than a cost. It is a liberation and a chance at individualized freedom, not just an oppressive routine.

Temple Grandin worries that today's world doesn't provide enough structured environments for autistics to flourish and that the modern workplace demands too much versatility. These are real concerns but I think the notion of a kinder, gentler time in earlier decades is largely a myth. Today we have more at-home production than ever before, we have more high-tech jobs, and we also have more niche jobs, design jobs, engineering jobs, math jobs, and jobs requiring lots of detailed focus.

The scope for division of labor in today's world, and the ongoing growth of that scope, is another reason why I don't identify autism—as a concept—with failed life outcomes. Whatever level of success autistics have achieved to date, there is a very good chance that level of success will rise. That's a prediction of Smithian economics.

Division of labor is not the only force supporting neurodiverse individuals in human society. Individual mobility, transportation, and globalization help autistics as well, even if many autistics are not themselves very mobile. When you live in a small village or hunter-gatherer society, everyone knows which people are considered to be "weird." They stick out like a sore thumb. But when I fly to, say, Dubai, hardly anyone knows whether or not I am weird. Perhaps I dress differently, talk differently, and spend too much time reading books, but to them I appear weird in any case. The proverbial "Aunt Millie from Peoria" also would come across as strange. The differences in weirdness are blurred, and those who would have been seen as weird at home can pass for simply being "foreign." Of course foreigners also come to the United States, whether to visit or immigrate, and that increases the public's general understanding of the overall diversity of the human race.

Yemen, which I have visited, is for the most part living in medieval conditions: virtually all the women I saw wore veils and all the men carried daggers and chewed the druglike khat. Just don't ask me who the weirdos were. I had no idea. But in my high school each person had a strong opinion about all of the others. It was hard to escape the tyranny of rigid classification. Overall the more mixed the crowd, and the greater the number of dimensions of status and achievement, the greater the chance that unusual people will find a means of excelling or just surviving or fitting in. To put it another way, the mixing of populations lowers the cost of being unusual. That's why gay people are especially likely to choose the coasts and major cities rather than small towns in the Midwest.

It's a common view in the autistic community that autistics, if they marry, are more likely to choose foreign spouses. When your partner is from another culture, the expectations for "fitting in" are looser and more flexible because the two people don't quite conform to traditional expectations in any case. That's another example of how trade and the diversity of modern society can benefit people with unusual or specialized cognitive abilities.

I was struck by a remark by Jonathan Sacks, the chief rabbi of Great Britain: "It is through exchange that difference becomes a blessing, not a curse." That's a message I hope this book has made clear. In this notion economics, neurology, and the web come together. The idea of trade—including trade with people of differing neurologies and cognitive abilities—is one reason why the web is so important. And it helps explain why trade is so important for autistic people in particular and how the rest of the world can benefit from autistic cognitive strengths by trading with autistics.

On a global scale, we are starting to see some cultural environments with elements sympathetic or conducive to autistics. Consider the otaku culture of Japan. Otaku culture is based on obsessive hobbies and interests, often of an obscure nature. These interests frequently involve gadgets and manga but they have grown in their diversity and today a Japanese otaku may develop an extreme focus on Humphrey Bogart movies, Brazilian pop music, or, to cite one notorious and increasingly mainstream example, women who dress up like maids. (If you are wondering, you study these women; you don't necessarily do anything with them.)

Japanese otaku are not generally autistic, the rate of measured autism in Japan does not seem to be higher than elsewhere, and many Japanese dislike otaku culture for its supposed weirdness. Nonetheless in Japan there is explicit recognition of hobbyist obsession as a way of life, not just as pathology. That recognition creates some cultural space for difference. Tokyo is a paradise for people with unusual or highly specialized interests. Given the efficiency of the Tokyo Metro, the city is in effect the world's biggest, richest, and most highly educated collection of consumers in one place. There's nothing else like it. You're supposed to obsess about things there and that's part of the charm of the place.

Japanese culture is also (unintentionally) autism-friendly in another way. The Japanese stress the idea of developing and fine-tuning a highly specialized skill over many years of precise training. That's why the Italian food in Japan is so good, even outside of the fine or expensive restaurants; the Japanese man cooking it probably had an apprenticeship in Italy for a few years and he has been perfecting his technique ever since. If you go to a restaurant in Japan serving Singaporean or Mexican food, the odds are that at least one person in the restaurant has done a true apprenticeship in the field. This kind of specialization is expected and indeed demanded. Temple Grandin once wrote: "I met a large number of high-functioning people on the autism spectrum [in Japan]. Every one of them was employed in a good job . . . What I noticed is that the attitude in Japan is to develop skills."

If you're doing a global tour of sites relevant to cultural diversity, think of Tokyo as stop number one. There is so much talk that Japan is such a homogeneous culture but in fact the place produces many hidden kinds of diversity. It's a shame that this Japanese innovation— the notion of otaku—isn't more widely recognized or assigned its proper importance. But still it represents a form of progress.

Next on the diversity tour is Finland, where high-tech jobs are common, the streets are remarkably quiet, the men are terse, contemporary classical music is popular, there is a visual rigor to the architecture, and it seems socially acceptable not to make eye contact when you speak to people. No, there is not scientific evidence that all those features are correlated with autism, but I am not the first person to notice that Finland offers many cultural features linked to autism in stereotypical fashion. Where did all those features come from? I have no idea, but the point is not to claim that the Finnish are all somehow secretly autistic. It is more likely that the specifics of some cultures evolve in directions more friendly to autism and autistics than others, albeit for reasons we do not understand.

I visited Finland once. It was the only time in my life that I felt like the resident extrovert, except perhaps for my trips on the Tokyo Metro.

When I saw a book entitled *Finland: Cultural Lone Wolf* after my visit, I could not help but buy it and read it the evening it arrived. I read:

Finns . . . have a desire for solitude.

Finns judge you by your degree of luotettavuus (reliability). There must be a strong word-deed correlation when you are dealing with them. Do what you have said you are going to do.

Finns are basically shy . . . in Finland one minds one's own business; gossip is frowned upon . . .

The first thing new arrivals in Finland are struck by is the taciturnity of Finnish males. The latter in turn are often put off by foreign loquacity and may react by retreating further into their shell.

Though Finns prefer to speak briefly, when they do open their mouths, they are generally very direct.

A Finnish male likes initial eye contact while introducing himself . . . but he avoids significant use of it after that.

The Finnish concept of time is almost exclusively monochromic. Good planners, they set out their immediate tasks in order of priority and begin solving them, pragmatically, one by one.

The book also notes that Finnish people do not like hearing more than one conversation at one time, a trait associated with many autistic people.

This is hardly rigorous evidence about Finnish society, but I did conclude that I should visit the country again.

For all those benefits there remains a big obstacle standing in the way of further progress. My fear is that many bigots and potential bigots are becoming better-educated about autism. Many autistics might in fact do better socially or in their careers if the world views them as "eccentrics" rather than as autistics. It is still a far from perfect world. If you think about the typical high-status image of a smart person, eccentric is OK and perhaps even prized. Loners are OK too, provided they are brilliant, extravagant, and unique. Ambiguity and opacity are valued, if only because people can speculate as to what really makes you tick. You can be an exotic man of mystery. But if what appeared to be eccentric is all of a sudden associated with the more generally available traits of a lower-status group ("disorders"), the smarts of the smart person are no longer framed so positively. "Oh, so it boils down to that" seems like such a deflating interpretation and it is a categorization that many people are afraid of. The result is that most of the smart and accomplished people don't want to have anything to do with the ideas of autism, Asperger's, and neurodiversity.

Whatever the tragedies in many autistic lives, autistic cognitive strengths have been vital to the progress of mankind and they are proving increasingly important for how we live and how we think, most of all when it comes to the web.

We need not just a better and deeper understanding of autism but we also need a stronger movement for true, respectful individualism for all human beings. That is my kind of happy ending, but it's not yet what we have in the world.

The final message of this book is not about autistics or any other group for that matter, and it's also not about the web. The final message of this book is about respect for the individual. The study of human neurology is important science, but it is not just science and it is not just a tool for diagnosis or medical intervention. It is also a path toward appreciating the diversity of the human spirit, the splendor of the individual mind, and the importance of respecting the individuality of each mind.

It's frequently been suggested that studying the human mind on a scientific basis will lead us to B. F. Skinner and his rats, to behaviorism and control, to fatalism, and to totalitarianism. I'm not convinced. The more we study the human mind, the more we can see the beauty and the uniqueness of the individual. General labels, such as "autistic," can be useful. But we need to remain aware of how much labels are imperfect substitutes for more detailed forms of knowledge about particular individuals. They are placeholders for a deeper understanding that is yet to come. And that's not just for the autistics.

Most so-called neurotypicals aren't typical at all and if we think they are it's because we don't yet appreciate their uniqueness in a sufficiently informed manner.

The deeper our understanding of human neurodiversity, and the deeper our appreciation for the individual, the more we can appreciate how many different ways the human mind can contemplate the beauty and wonder of creation. That sounds a bit corny but yes, it is part of the happy ending of this book.

Finally, maybe the happy ending—insofar as we have one—extends far beyond the planet where we live.

Perhaps interiority—my word for internal mental existence—is to be found not only among autistics, in new technologies, and on the internet. Interiority may be part of the very fabric of the universe around us. That sounds odd but it makes sense if you spend some time pondering what is called the Fermi Paradox. This conundrum, a popular topic of discussion among the philosophically inclined, is named after Enrico Fermi, a physicist and one of the creative forces behind the construction of the atomic bomb.

If I look outside, toward the rest of the universe, I am struck by the apparent absence of signs of intelligent life. Apart from human beings and the other intelligent animals on this planet, we don't see signs of intelligence in our galaxy. As Fermi himself asked: "Where are they?"

Nevertheless, the more we study our immediate region of the universe, the more we find a large number of solar systems with planets. As of March 2008, there were 277 confirmed extra-solar planets and we are finding more all the time. There are maybe 250 billion stars right here in our Milky Way. It seems that even Alpha Centauri, the star nearest to our sun, has planets, and possibly Earth-like planets. The more we look at these planets in our galaxy, the more some of them seem to resemble Earth, or at least seem like they might possibly resemble Earth. That means there is some chance they harbor intelligent life. I also can imagine that intelligent life could evolve on planets that don't much look like Earth but have, say, oceans of methane or other gases. Even if I am wrong in that speculation, the overall number of possibilities for intelligent life is impressively and unexpectedly high.

We know that intelligent life is possible in the first place, given that we find intelligent life here on Earth. And intelligence has evolved in a number of species, not just in human beings. Whales, chimpanzees, elephants, crows, and ravens all seem to be smart in their own ways. They're not smart enough or physically endowed enough to build technologically sophisticated civilizations, but their multiple existences reflect the survival value of intelligence in a biological setting. Once the door is opened for intelligence, it seems that some intelligences, albeit not all, will evolve into advanced civilizations.

I've seen interesting calculations as to how many intelligent civilizations should be out there in the galaxy. This is sometimes called the Drake Equation.

The Drake Equation states that:

$$N = N^* \times f_p \times n_e \times f_l \times f_i \times f_c \times f_L$$

In that equation N^* represents the number of stars in the Milky Way Galaxy, f_p is the percentage of stars that have planets around them, n_e is the number of planets per star that can sustain life, f_l is the fraction of planets where life evolves, f_i is the fraction of life-bearing planets with intelligent life, f_c is the fraction of f_i that communicates, and f_L is the fraction of the planet's life during which communicating civilizations are active. Multiplying all those variables will give us the left-hand side of the equation, N, or the number of communicating civilizations in the galaxy.

Even under relatively pessimistic assumptions, the Drake Equation implies there should be many advanced civilizations. You can tinker with those numbers for hours, but it is very hard to get the right answer to come about as only 1, namely human civilization. And insofar as we are learning more about the numbers, such as when we discover new planets in other solar systems, the prospects for intelligent life elsewhere are rising, not falling. So to repeat Fermi's question: Where are they?

It doesn't have to be little green men visiting on our doorstep. It seems that an advanced civilization would have many ways to leave traces of its presence. They could send radio signals with frequencies corresponding to commonly recognized mathematical numbers, such as pi (3.14 . . .) or e, the natural logarithm (2.716 . . .). Or how about self-replicating, solar-powered space probes to circle observed planets? Given the (supposed) number of intelligent alien civilizations, you don't have to think that any one of these forms of greeting is especially likely. A technology of greeting has only to succeed once in reaching us. What is striking is that we are receiving no greetings or at least we are not able to recognize such greetings.

Is it possible that advanced civilizations could manipulate sections of the galaxy to make their presence visible at a great distance? Imagine stars, or other light sources, arrayed in unusual and highly visible patterns or emitting unusual frequencies. Call them advanced stellar artifacts. We would get the message. Again, it has to happen only once. But no alien government or alien philanthropist seems to have taken an interest in such a project. I am surprised that we do not see some forms of interstellar advertising; after all is not the sky an ideal way to reach consumers (if I may call them that) across the galaxy? We've even started sending ads ourselves, albeit in very basic form. In June 2008, a group of Norwegian astronomers broadcast a Doritos ad to a distant star, forty-two light years away.

One possible conclusion is simply that advanced, intelligent life is extremely rare in our part of the universe. Maybe, but that is at odds with the fact of our existence. We only have to develop human civilization a bit further before we can ourselves seed the galaxy with robots or messages or space probes or whatever. We could send word of who we are and what we can do, and if we are so close to that point why should we be the only ones to reach that stage?

Alternatively, we might believe that advanced civilizations collapse very quickly. Maybe intelligent life is common but catastrophe kicks in, whether because of an errant asteroid or internecine warfare or environmental collapse or some other factor we do not yet understand. Of course if that is your view, you shouldn't be too optimistic about the future of humanity. That's one way to end up in a very unhappy ending.

But I find another explanation of this silence more plausible, namely interiority. Perhaps advanced civilizations are not very exhibitionistic but instead they look to perfect their interior dimensions. They look for happiness, understanding, order, profundity, and beauty, and they find all of these qualities internally. At some level of technology there is no point to building bigger structures or manipulating exploding stars. After all, if your civilization is advanced enough, what is the point of size?

Rather than making themselves bigger and more visible, advanced civilizations may try to make themselves smaller, less visible, and thus more robust. These civilizations will devote their wisdom and energies to digging inward and exploring the life of the mind. After all, it is bigger, expansionistic civilizations that are going to collide or serve as targets for more advanced competitors. Perhaps galactic evolution and competition favor the small, just as insects seem to be doing so well here on planet Earth. What about the notion of a "civilization" that uses information and energy so efficiently that it can fit inside the head of a pin or an even smaller space? We wouldn't expect to find a visible trace of their existence.

Many people overlook this possibility precisely because they expect to find intelligence in familiar forms and in familiar packages. In fact it's a bit like how the cognitive strengths of autistic people, especially those who do not behave according to mainstream standards in mainstream society, are overlooked.

One anonymous commentator on my blog, www.marginalrevolution.com, had an interesting hypothesis in response to a post of mine about the Fermi Paradox. He or she predicted:

> Sufficiently advanced civilizations probably become utterly dependent on pervasive low-latency communications protocols, such that their members need to permanently remain within a fraction of a light-second's distance from one another. Think Facebook and mobile phones on steroids . . .

Uploaded beings will probably live accelerated lives: they will have a much higher clock speed, because electronic or photonic devices run much faster than the chemical reactions that power an organic brain . . . due to speed-of-light issues, their entire civilizations may be constrained to exist within a sphere of a few hundred meters in radius or less. Their civilizations may also have short life spans: an epic rise and fall of many millennia of subjective time may take place within a few days of real time.

. . . perhaps sufficiently intelligent life inevitably bootstraps itself into some entirely different form. We might be like a fetus floating alone inside a womb and wondering, where is everybody?

That's a pretty exotic set of hypotheses, but I like the basic ideas, namely that a) human beings are just getting started, b) the most advanced civilizations will have a largely mental existence, and c) those civilizations will find their highest fulfillment in the notion of "Facebook on steroids."

So when we look up into the stars, we can choose among different feelings. On the sadder side, we can see emptiness and feel destruction and loss. But when I look up at the sky and gaze at the stars, I am joyful. I see a happy ending. I see interiority.

It is the secret of the best kind of prosperity, no matter how disordered you find the world. It is the secret of creating your own economy.

FURTHER READING AND REFERENCES

CHAPTER 1: THE FUTURE OF THINKING DIFFERENTLY

On Mark Donohoo, see "One Man's Story: When an Autistic Child Grows Up," April 1, 2008, www.cnn.com/2008/HEALTH/conditions/04/01/autism.jeffs.story/index.html.

For the story of Ethan, see Michael D. Powers and Janet Poland, *Asperger Syndrome and Your Child: A Parent's Guide* (New York: Collins Living, 2003), chapter 2.

To the best of my knowledge, the phrase "infovores" originates with USC professor Irving Biederman.

For a good presentation of framing effects, see for instance Richard H. Thaler and Cass R. Sunstein, *Nudge: Improving Decisions About Health, Wealth, and Happiness* (New Haven: Yale University Press, 2008).

For the Steve Hofstetter quotation, see "Thinking Man: Steve Hofstetter is Your Friend," November 14, 2005, www.collegehumor.com/article:1632255.

On "Facebook-like" services for the very young, see Camille Sweeney, "Twittering from the Cradle," *The New York Times,* September 11, 2008.

For sources on Google Earth, see the Google Earth blog, www.gearthblog.com/blog/archives/2007/10/new_youtube_layer_in_google_earth.html. On crashing pools, see James Sherwood, "Teens Use Technology to Party in Neighbors' Pools," June 18, 2008, www.reghardware.co.uk/2008/06/18/tech_aids_pool_crashing/.

On the precise ordering of physical daily experience, see Monica Hesse, "Bytes of Life," *Washington Post,* September 9, 2008.

The interview with Kamran Nazeer is taken from the blog of Seth Roberts, www.blog.sethroberts.net/2008/04/05/interview-with-kamran-nazeer-part-1/.

CHAPTER 2: HIDDEN CREATIVITY

For one good discussion of the difference between cognitive and behavioral differences in autism, see the discussion by Anne C. found here online: www.existenceiswonderful.com/2008/09/conceptualizing-autism.html. For general discussions on autism and how it is treated in popular discourse, see Paul A. Offit, *Autism's False Prophets: Bad Science, Risky Medicine, and the Search for a Cure* (New York: Columbia University Press, 2008).

On autism per se I recommend Fred R. Volkmar, Rhea Paul, Ami Klin, and Donald Cohen, eds., *Handbook of Autism and Pervasive Developmental Disorders,* vol. 1 (Hoboken, NJ: John Wiley & Sons, 2005), and also Dermot Bowler, *Autism Spectrum Disorders: Psychological Theory and Research* (West Sussex: John Wiley & Sons, 2007), noting that they are dense in presentation. A good place to follow research on autism is the *Journal of Autism and Developmental Disorders;* Francesca Happé's 1994 book *Autism: An Introduction to Psychological Theory* (Cambridge, MA: Harvard University Press, 1998) is useful for framing many points. On a more popular level, I very much recommend Douglas Biklen's collection of writings by autistics, *Autism and the Myth of the Person Alone* (New York: New York University Press, 2005). The autism blogging of Kristina Chew is another good source of information. The works of Temple Grandin have been very important and influential; see for instance her *Thinking in Pictures, Expanded Edition: My Life with Autism* (New York: Vintage, 2006).

On the lesser susceptibility of autistics to some optical illusions and their superior skills in spotting some kinds of patterns, see Dermot M. Bowler, *Autism Spectrum Disorders: Psychological Theory and Research* (cited above), chapter 5. On visual acuity, see for instance Emma Ashwin, Chris Ashwin, Danielle Rhydderch, Jessica Howells, and Simon Baron-Cohen, "Eagle-Eyed Visual Acuity: An Experimental Investigation of Enhanced Perception in Autism," *Biological Psychiatry* 65, no. 1 (January 2009), 17–21.

Chapter 6 of the Dermot Bowler book covers some autistic cognitive strengths in attention and perception, including auditory perception. See also the later discussion of music in chapter 8 of this book and other discussions in the chapters to follow.

On autism and the bias toward local perception, see for instance Francesca Happé and Uta Frith, "The Weak Coherence Account: Detail-Focused Cognitive Style in Autism Spectrum Disorders," *Journal of Autism and Developmental Disorders* 36, no. 1 (January 2006), 5–25, and also Rhonda Booth, Rebecca Charlton, Claire Hughes, and Francesca Happé, "Disentangling Weak Coherence and Executive Dysfunction: Planning Drawing in Autism and Attention-Deficit/Hyperactivity Disorder," *Philosophical Transactions: Biological Sciences* (February 28, 2003), 387–92. See also Beatriz López and Susan R. Leekam, "Do Children with Autism Fail to Process Information in Context?" *Journal of Child Psychology and Psychiatry* 44, no. 2 (2003), 285–300; this piece shows that local processing need not involve a disregard for context and the bigger picture.

For a survey of the growing literature on the cognitive strengths of autism, see Michelle Dawson, Laurent Mottron, and Morton Ann Gernsbacher, "Learning in Autism," in J. H. Bryne (series editor) and H. Roediger (volume editor), *Learning and Memory: A Comprehensive Reference* (New York: Elsevier, 2008). On whether autism necessarily involves a defective "executive function," see Miriam Liss and Deborah Fein, Carl Feinstein, Lynn Waterhouse, Doris Allen and Michelle Dunn, Robin Morris, and Isabelle Rapin,

"Executive Functioning in High-Functioning Children with Autism," *Journal of Child Psychology and Psychiatry* 42, no. 2 (2001), 261–70.

On the perceptual and sensory sensitivities of autistics, see for instance Grace T. Baranek, Fabian J. David, Michele D. Poe, Wendy L. Stone, and Linda R. Watson, "Sensory Experiences Questionnaire: Discriminating Sensory Features in Young Children with Autism, Developmental Delays, and Typical Development," *Journal of Child Psychology and Psychiatry* 47, no. 6 (2006), 591–601.

On whether autistics suffer from the lack of a "theory of mind" or whether this is simply picking up speech deficits or other cognitive problems, see for instance Morton Ann Gernsbacher and Jennifer L. Frymiare, "Does the Autistic Brain Lack Core Modules?" *Journal of Developmental and Learning Disorders* 9 (2005), 3–16. See also Lawrence Hirschfeld, Elizabeth Bartmess, Sarah White, and Uta Frith, "Can autistic children predict by social stereotypes?" *Current Biology* 17, no. 12 (June 19, 2007), 451–52. It turns out that yes, autistic children can predict social behavior in this way.

On the view that Asperger's syndrome is simply a form of autism, one good article is Jonathan M. Campbell, "Diagnostic Assessment of Asperger's Disorder: A Review of Five Third-Party Rating Scales," *Journal of Autism and Developmental Disorders* 35, no. 1 (February 2005), 25–35. See also Kathleen E. Macintosh and Cheryl Dissanayake, "Annotation: The Similarities and Differences Between Autistic Disorder and Asperger's Disorder: A Review of the Empirical Evidence," *Journal of Child Psychology and Psychiatry* 45, no. 3 (2004), 421–34.

On Craig Newmark and Asperger's, see www.cnewmark.com/2003/09/craigslist_docu.html.

On Bram Cohen, see Susan Berfield, "Do I Look Like a CEO?" *BusinessWeek,* October 27, 2008, 46–49.

See Thomas Sowell, *Late-Talking Children* (New York: Basic Books, 1997), and also Sowell's *The Einstein Syndrome: Bright Children Who Talk Late* (New York: Basic Books, 2002).

On "recovery" from autism, see Molly Helt, Elizabeth Kelley, Marcel Kins-bourne, Juhi Pandey, Hilary Borstein, Martha Herbert, and Deborah Fein, "Can Children with Autism Recover? If So, How?" *Neuropsychology Review* 18 (2008), 339–66. For the quotation from Fein with the estimate of 20 per-cent, see Jayne Lytel, "My Son Was Autistic: Is He Still?" *Washington Post,* November 18, 2008. On the instability of early autism diagnoses, see Lauren M. Turner and Wendy L. Stone, "Variability in outcome for children with an ASD diagnosis at age 2," *Journal of Child Psychology and Psychiatry* 48 (2007), 793–802.

On Michelle Dawson and the Ravens I.Q. test, see Michelle Dawson, Isa-belle Soulières, Morton Ann Gernsbacher, and Laurent Mottron, "The Level and Nature of Autistic Intelligence," *Psychological Science* 18, no. 8 (2007), 657–62.

The Belmonte quotation is from his essay "The Yellow Raincoat," in Sherry Turkle, ed., *Evocative Objects: Things We Think With* (Cambridge, MA: The MIT Press, 2007), 73.

The quotations from Joshua Kendall's book on Roget, *The Man Who Made Lists: Love, Death, Madness, and the Creation of Roget's Thesaurus* (New York: G.P. Putnam's Sons, 2008), are from pp. 39, 40, and 277.

In the Buffett biography, see Alice Schroeder, *The Snowball: Warren Buffett and the Business of Life* (New York: Bantam, 2008), 53, 137, passim.

On autistics and humor, see Victoria Lyons and Michael Fitzgerald, "Humor in Autism and Asperger's Syndrome," *Journal of Autism and Developmental Disorders* 34, no. 5 (October 2004), 521–31.

The Dr. Sandi Chapman quotation can be found in "UTD Docs Use Online World to Treat Form of Autism," July 9, 2008, cbs11tv.com/local/aspergers .syndrome.treatment.2.767511.html.

The Jim Sinclair passage is from "Some Thoughts About Empathy," web.syr .edu/%7Ejisincla/empathy.htm. Jason Seneca's words are from his essay "An

Aspie's Guide to Everyone Else," in *Voices of Autism: The Healing Companion: Stories for Courage, Comfort and Strength,* edited by The Healing Project (New York: LaChance Publishing, 2008), 113–18; see p. 117.

For a debunking of the claim that autistics lack compassion, see Morton Ann Gernsbacher, "Toward a Behavior of Reciprocity," currently at psych.wisc .edu/lang/pdf/gernsbacher_reciprocity.pdf, and also Kimberley Rogers, Isabel Dziobek, Jason Hassenstab, Oliver T. Wolf, and Antonio Convit, "Who Cares? Revisiting Empathy in Asperger's Syndrome," *Journal of Autism and Developmental Disorders* 37, no. 4 (April 2007), 709–15.

On the complex question of which early traits predict successful and unsuccessful autistic outcomes, such as intelligence or later achievement, see Patricia Howlin, "Outcomes in Autism Spectrum Disorders," *Handbook of Autism and Pervasive Developmental Disorders* (cited above), 201–22. See also P. Szatmari, G. Bartolucci, R. Brenner, S. Bond, and S. Rich, "A Follow-Up Study of High-Functioning Autistic Children," *Journal of Autism and Developmental Disorders* 19, no. 2 (1989), 213–25. This issue remains unresolved.

On *The New York Times,* see for instance Liesl Schillinger, "Who Do You Love?" July 13, 2008, and also David Brooks, "The Rank-Link Imbalance," March 14, 2008. I nonetheless remain very much a fan of both of these excellent writers.

The Ganz essay is in Steven O. Moldin and John L. R. Rubenstein, eds., *Understanding Autism: From Basic Neuroscience to Treatment* (New York: Taylor and Francis, 2006). The Bainbridge book is *Beyond the Zonules of Zinn* (Cambridge, MA: Harvard University Press, 2008); see p. 283.

On how parents of autistic children show some partially autistic traits, see the work of Simon Baron-Cohen, for instance Simon Baron-Cohen, Sally Wheelwright, Amy Burtenshaw, and Esther Hobson, "Mathematical Talent is Linked to Autism," in *Human Nature,* forthcoming; it is currently on the web at www.autismresearchcentre.com/docs/papers/2007_BC_etal_maths.pdf.

The Centre for Autism Research is a good source for many of Baron-Cohen's papers on related topics.

See also on genetics J. Briskman, U Frith, and F. Happé, "Exploring the Cognitive Phenotype of Autism: Weak 'Central Coherence' in Parents and Siblings of Children with Autism: II. Real-life Skills and Preferences," *Journal of Child Psychology and Psychiatry and Allied Disciplines* 42 (2001), 309–16. On some of the genetic issues behind autism, see Michael Rutter, "Genetic Influences and Autism," *Handbook of Autism and Pervasive Developmental Disorders* (cited above), 425–52. Recent pieces include Brett S. Abrahams and Daniel H. Geschwind, "Advances in autism genetics: On the threshold of a new neurobiology," *Nature Reviews Genetics* 9, May 2008, 341–55, and Molly Losh, Patrick F. Sullivan, Dimitri Trembath, and Joseph Piven, "Current Developments in the Genetics of Autism: From Phenome to Genome," *Journal of Neuropathology and Experimental Neurology* 67, no. 9 (September 2008), 829–37.

The transmission of autism usually is rooted in multiple genes in some complex fashion (i.e., idiopathic autism), again with the possibility of environmental triggers. Some less common forms of autism—etiological autism—have specific causes or associations, such as the chromosomal defects behind "fragile X syndrome."

On epidemiology, see Eric Fombonne, "Epidemiological Studies of Pervasive Developmental Disorders," in *Handbook of Autism and Developmental Disorders*, 3rd edition, vol. 1: "Diagnosis, Development, Neurobiology, and Behavior," edited by Fred R. Volkmar, Rhea Paul, Ami Klin, and Donald Cohen (Hoboken, NJ: John Wiley & Sons, 2005), 42–69.

One study of autism as a spectrum is Maj-Britt Posserud, Astri J. Landervold, and Christopher Gilberg, "Autistic Features in a Total Population of 7–9-year-old Children Assessed by the ASSQ," *Journal of Child Psychology and Psychiatry* 47, no. 2 (2006), 167–75. This area remains underexplored but it has been attracting more attention.

CHAPTER 3: WHY MODERN CULTURE IS LIKE MARRIAGE, IN ALL ITS GLORY

On short bits, see Susan Jacoby, *The Age of American Unreason* (New York: Pantheon Books, 2008), 257–59. On radio ads and YouTube, see Seth Godin, *Meatball Sundae: Is Your Marketing Out of Sync?* (New York: Portfolio, 2007), pp. 96–100. The web page with information about short bits is called "Short Is In": kk.org/ct2/2008/03/short-is-in.php.

On the top websites, see www.alexa.com/site/ds/top_500.

On the Flynn Effect, see for instance James T. Flynn, *What Is Intelligence? Beyond the Flynn Effect* (Cambridge, UK: Cambridge University Press, 2007).

For the essay by Mark Bittman, see "I Need a Virtual Break. No, Really," *New York Times,* March 2, 2008.

On the notion of filter failure, see "Interview with Clay Shirky, Part I," *Columbia Journalism Review,* December 19, 2008, www.cjr.org/overload/interview_with_clay_shirky_par.php, as well as Shirky's work more generally.

On improved productivity in task-switching, see Meredith Minear and Priti Shah, "Task switching training and transfer in two switching paradigms: Transferable improvement in global, but not local switch costs," *Memory & Cognition* 36 (2008), 1470–83.

For a discussion of Twist and Twitter, see Jason Kottke's blog, www.kottke.org/08/10/twitter-trends.

CHAPTER 4: IM, CELL PHONES, AND FACEBOOK

My favorite Harold Innis book is *The Bias of Communication,* second ed. (Toronto: University of Toronto Press, 2008). For Leonard Dudley see *The Word and the Sword: How Techniques of Information and Violence Have Shaped Our World* (Oxford: Blackwell, 1991).

The IM exchange is cited in Christine Lee, "How Does Instant Messaging Affect Interaction Between the Genders?" currently at www.stanford.edu/class/pwr3-25/group2/pdfs/IM_Genders.pdf.

On the letter "C," see "The Internet: Communication Corruptor or Language Liberator?" *Journal of Young Investigators,* www.jyi.org/features/ft.php?id=258.

On IM and workplace interruptions, see *Science Daily,* "Instant Messaging Proves Useful in Reducing Workplace Interruptions," June 4, 2008, www.sciencedaily.com/releases/2008/06/080603120251.htm.

For some of the material on text messaging, see Donna and Fraser Reid, "Insights into the Social and Psychological Effects of Text Messaging," University of Plymouth working paper, 2004, www.160characters.org/documents/SocialEffectsOfTextMessaging.pdf.

On fleshmeets, see "Family Ties: Kith and kin get closer, with consequences for strangers," *Economist,* April 12–18, 2008, 11–15, special supplement on mobile telecoms.

On the analogy between twittering and a bar conversation, see confusedofcalcutta.com/2007/12/23/a-sideways-look-at-twitter-in-the-enterprise/.

On Frederic Brochet and the wine experiments and related work, see Jonah Lehrer, "Grape Expectations: What Wine Can Tell Us About the Nature of Reality," *Boston Globe,* February 24, 2008.

For Adam Smith on social validation, see *The Theory of Moral Sentiments,* part 3.

On self-similarity, see Stephanie Rosenbloom, "Names That Match Forge a Bond on the Internet," *The New York Times,* April 10, 2008.

CHAPTER 5: THE BUDDHA AS SAVIOR AND THE PROFESSOR AS SHAMAN

For a few of the more serious works on Buddhism in the English language, see for instance John Powers, *Introduction to Tibetan Buddhism* (Ithaca, NY: Snow Lion Publications, 1995), Reginald A. Ray, *Secret of the Vajra World: The Tantric Buddhism of Tibet* (Boston: Shambhala, 2001), and David Gordon White, ed., *Tantra in Practice* (Princeton: Princeton University Press, 2000). For an interesting treatment integrating the Buddhist concept of mindfulness with neurology, see Daniel J. Siegel, *The Mindful Brain: Reflection and Attunement in the Cultivation of Well-Being* (New York: W.W. Norton, 2007). Chris Mitchell's recent *Asperger's Syndrome and Mindfulness* (London and Philadelphia: Jessica Kingsley Publishers, 2009) considers what AS individuals might learn from Buddhism.

For the account of Sue Rubin, see her fascinating essay "A Conversation with Leo Kanner" in Douglas Biklen, ed., *Autism and the Myth of the Person Alone* (New York: New York University Press, 2005).

The Perry Mehrling biography of Fischer Black is *Fischer Black and the Revolutionary Idea of Finance* (New York: Wiley, 2005); see pp. 245–46. The Ed Boyden blog post can be found at Ed Boyden's blog: "How to Think: Managing Brain Resources in an Age of Complexity," November 13, 2007, www.technologyreview.com/blog/boyden/21925/.

For one discussion of MyLifeBits, see www.marginalrevolution.com/marginal revolution/2007/02/in_case_you_for.html.

The best place to read about the debates on Wikipedia and classification is meta.wikipedia.org.

The Keillor anecdote is taken from a web article on the psychology of collecting; see boards.collectors-society.com/ubbthreads.php/ubb/showflat/Number/-1449381/site_id/1#import, in turn drawn from Steve Winn, "Call them what you will—obsessive compulsive eccentrics, materialist philosophers or packrat artists—collectors' 'unruly passions' make sense of our world," *San Francisco Chronicle*, December 15, 2003.

The Fauron quotation is from Jean Baudrillard, *The System of Objects* (London: Verso Books, 1996), 94.

On George Veley, see Rolf Potts, "Mister Universe: What Makes Someone Want to Be the World's Most Traveled Man?" *New York Times Magazine*, November 16, 2008, 84–87.

The educational test questions are from Charles Murray's *Real Education: Four Simple Truths for Bringing America's Schools Back to Reality* (New York: Crown Forum, 2008), 36–37.

On daydreaming and mental resting states in autism, see Daniel P. Kennedy, Elizabeth Redcay, and Eric Courchesne, "Failing to deactivate: resting functional abnormalities in autism," *Proceedings of the National Academy of Sciences* 103, no. 21 (May 23, 2006), 8275–80.

The greater focus of autistics does require qualification. Often the autistic can be less focused if they are distracted and in some regards they are more easily distracted than non-autistics; remember the discussion of the startle reaction? For a discussion of this issue, see Dermot Bowler, *Autism Spectrum Disorders: Psychological Theory and Research* (cited above), 115–17. In any case, one can think of neurotypicals as trying, through education, to attain the non-distracted maximum focus found in many autistics.

For the Department of Education figure, see www.ed.gov/about/overview/budget/budget03/summary/appl/edlite-index.html.

CHAPTER 6: THE NEW ECONOMY OF STORIES

You'll find Schelling's essay in his *Choice and Consequence: Perspectives of an Errant Economist* (Cambridge, MA: Harvard University Press, 1984). On stories I am also much influenced by Pascal Boyer's *Religion Explained* (New York: Basic Books, 2002) and William Flesch's *Comeuppance: Costly*

Signaling, Altruistic Punishment, and Other Biological Components of Fiction (Cambridge, MA: Harvard University Press, 2008). Also important is Eduardo Gianetti's *Lives We Live By: The Art of Self Deception* (London: Bloomsbury, 2001).

The Pessoa quotation is from Fernando Pessoa, *The Book of Disquiet* (New York: Penguin Books, 1998), 252. Pessoa offers many ideas of interest for this book.

On the García Márquez title, the original Spanish is *La vida no es la que uno vivío, sino la que uno recuerda y cómo la recuerda para contarla.*

On the role of scarcity in the Harry Potter stories, see Megan McArdle, "Harry Potter: The Economics," *Guardian,* July 20, 2007, www.guardian.co .uk/commentisfree/2007/jul/20/harrypottertheeconomics.

For the Dante quotation, see *Paradiso,* canto XXIV, 25–27, translated by Robert and Jean Hollander (New York: Anchor Books, 2007).

On weaker personal episodic memory in autism, see for instance Sophie Lind and Dermot Bowler, "Episodic memory and autonoetic consciousness in autistic spectrum disorders: The roles of self-awareness, representational abilities and temporal cognition," in *Memory in Autism,* edited by Jill Boucher and Dermot Bowler (Cambridge, UK: Cambridge University Press, 2008), 66–187.

On autism and stories, see for instance Rosa M. Garcia Perez, R. Peter Hobson, and Anthony Lee, "Narrative Role-Taking in Autism," *Journal of Autism and Developmental Disorders* 38, no. 1 (January 2008), 156–68. On dreams, see for instance Anne-Marie Daoust, Félix-Antoine Lusignan, Claude M. J. Braun, Laurent Mottron, and Roger Godbout, "Dream Content Analysis in Persons with an Autism Spectrum Disorder," *Journal of Autism and Developmental Disorders* 38, no. 4 (April 2008), 634–43. For an extreme (and I think exaggerated) view on autism and stories, see Matthew K. Belmonte, "Human, but More So: What the Autistic Brain Tells Us about the Process of

Narrative," in *Autism and Representation*, edited by Mark Osteen (New York: Routledge, 2008), 166–79.

The Jim Sinclair passage is from "Some Thoughts About Empathy," web.syr .edu/%7Ejisincla/empathy.htm.

The CNN.com story is Madison Park, "Looking for Hope in the Ashes," November 19, 2008, www.cnn.com/2008/HEALTH/conditions/11/18/autism .california.fire/index.html.

The Pessoa quotation is from p. 153 of Fernando Pessoa, *The Book of Disquiet* (New York: Penguin Books, 1998).

CHAPTER 7: HEROES

For the actual citations to the Sherlock Holmes stories, I have found it easier to keep the direct citations in the text. All citations are to the edition *Sherlock Holmes: The Complete Novels and Stories,* vols. 1 and 2 (New York: Bantam Dell, 2003).

Michael Fitzgerald, *The Genesis of Artistic Creativity: Asperger's Syndrome and the Arts* (Philadelphia: Jessica Kingsley Publishers, 2005), chapter 6, is the main source discussing the connections between Doyle, Holmes, and Asperger's. For an argument that characters in Jane Austen novels lie along the autistic spectrum, see Phyllis Ferguson Bottomer, *So Odd a Mixture: Along the Autistic Spectrum in* Pride and Prejudice (Philadelphia: Jessica Kingsley Publishers, 2007).

On mail to Holmes and the popularity of the character, see en.wikipedia.org/ wiki/221B_Baker_Street. On the Sherlock Holmes societies, see Russell Miller, *The Adventures of Arthur Conan Doyle* (London: Harvill Secker, 2008), 4.

For discussions of Holmes's methods of reasoning, see Umberto Eco and Thomas A. Sebeok, eds., *The Sign of Three: Dupin, Holmes, Peirce* (Bloomington: Indiana University Press, 1983). See also Michael Atkinson, *The Secret*

Marriage of Sherlock Holmes and Other Eccentric Readings (Ann Arbor: University of Michigan Press, 1996), 107. For Doyle's discussion of the Holmes character within himself, see his autobiography *Memories and Adventures* (Boston: Little, Brown, and Company, 1924), 94–95, and on Adrian Conan Doyle's description of his father, see Adrian Conan Doyle, *The True Conan Doyle* (New York: Coward-McCann, 1946), 18–19, and also Samuel Rosenberg, *Naked Is the Best Disguise: The Death and Resurrection of Sherlock Holmes* (New York: Penguin Books, 1974), 15–16. On the private interview, see Trevor H. Hall, *Sherlock Holmes and His Creator* (New York: St. Martin's Press, 1977), 87–88, plus the Adrian Conan Doyle book. See also Pierre Nordon, *Conan Doyle: A Biography* (New York: Holt, Rinehart, and Winston, 1967), chapter 15.

The standard English-language edition of Hesse, from which I have drawn page numbers, is Hermann Hesse, *The Glass Bead Game: A Novel* (New York: Picador, 2002). For an account of Hesse's childhood meltdowns, see also Ralph Freedman, *Hermann Hesse: Pilgrim of Crisis* (New York: Pantheon Books, 1978), chapter 1. For other biographical information on Hesse, see Richard C. Helt, *". . . A Poet or Nothing At All": The Tübingen and Basel Years of Hermann Hesse* (Providence: Berghahn Books, 1996), 21–22 (the quotation from the father is from p. 21), and see also Ralph Freedman, *Hermann Hesse* (cited above), 46–48.

One book that "plays the diagnosis game" is Michael Fitzgerald and Brendan O'Brien, *Genius Genes: How Asperger Talents Changed the World* (Shawnee Mission, KS: APC, 2007). On Glenn Gould, see Peter F. Ostwald, *Glenn Gould: The Ecstasy and Tragedy of Genius* (New York: W. W. Norton and Co., 1997).

On Adam Smith's view of *The Theory of Moral Sentiments,* see Ian Simpson Ross, *The Life of Adam Smith* (Oxford: Clarendon Press, 1995), 177.

For various pieces of biographical information on Smith, see adamsmithslostle gacy.com/2008/03/adam-smith-and-tourettes-syndrome.html. On Stewart, see William Robert Scott, *Adam Smith as Student and Professor* (New York: Augustus M. Kelley, 1965), 77. The John Rae quotation is from John Rae, *Life of*

Adam Smith, chapter 17, online at www.econlib.org/library/YPDBooks/Rae/raeLS17.html#Chapter%2017. And from Stewart, see Dugald Stewart, "Account of the Life and Writings of Adam Smith," republished in W.P.D. Wightman and J. C. Bryce, eds., *Adam Smith: Essays on Philosophical Subjects* (Indianapolis: Liberty Classics, 1976), 330. Note also that Vernon Smith, in *Rationality in Economics: Constructivist and Ecological Forms* (Cambridge, UK: Cambridge University Press, 2007), 18–19, speculates on a link between Smith and Asperger's.

On Jared Blackburn, Jared is autistic and the discussion is from Autism Europe's Conference 2000. You will find the discussion here: autistics.org/library/AE2000-ToM.html; an incomplete print reference is given as well: J. Blackburn, K. Gottschewski, Elsa George, and Niki L, "A Discussion About Theory of Mind: From an Autistic Perspective," *Proceedings of Autism Europe's Sixth International Congress,* Glasgow, Scotland, May 19–21, 2000. Currently an online version is here: www.autistics.org/library/AE2000-ToM.html.

On Smith and distance, I am indebted to an unpublished paper by Maria Pia Paganelli of Yeshiva University, namely "The Moralizing Role of Distance in Adam Smith," 2008.

CHAPTER 8: BEAUTY ISN'T WHAT YOU THINK IT IS

On Kiriana Cowansage, see Carlin Fiora, "An Aspie in the City," *Psychology Today,* November/December 2006. Accessed online: http://www.psychologytoday.com/articles/index.php?term=pto-4197.html&fromMod=emailed.

On music and neurology, some useful sources are John A. Sloboda, *The Musical Mind: The Cognitive Psychology of Music* (Oxford: Clarendon Press, 1985), and David Temperly, *The Cognition of Basic Musical Structures* (Cambridge, MA: MIT Press, 2001)

On amusia, see the work of Isabelle Peretz, for instance her online paper "Musical Disorders from Behavior to Genes," www.psychologicalscience.org/journals/cd/17_5_inpress/Peretz.pdf.

On autism and pitch, see Pamela Heaton, Kerry Williams, Omar Cummins, and Francesca Happé, "Autism and pitch processing splinter skills: A group and subgroup analysis," *Autism* 12, no. 2 (2008), 203–19. See also Anna Bonnel, Laurent Mottron, Isabelle Peretz, Manon Trudel, Erick Gallun, and Anne-Marie Bonnel, "Enhanced Pitch Sensitivity in Individuals with Autism: A Signal Detection Analysis," *Journal of Cognitive Neuroscience* 15, no. 2 (2003), 226–35.

On the correlation between perfect pitch and eccentrics, see Walter A. Brown, Karen Commuso, Henry Sachs, Brian Winklosky, Julie Mullane, Raphael Bernier, Sarah Svenson, Deborah Arin, Beth Rosen-Sheidley, and Susan E. Folstein, "Autism-Related Language, Personality, and Cognition in People with Absolute Pitch: Results of a Preliminary Study," *Journal of Autism and Developmental Disorders* 33, no. 2 (April 2003), 163–67.

On the fact that autistics do not show below-average ability to perceive "affect" in music, see P. Heaton, B. Hermelin, and L. Pring, "Can children with autistic spectrum disorders perceive affect in music? An experimental investigation," *Psychological Medicine* 29, no. 6 (1999), 1405–10.

See Rebecca Delaney, "Music critic describes life with Asperger's syndrome," *Columbia Missourian,* March 13, 2008, www.columbiamissourian.com/stories/2008/03/13/music-critic-describes-life-wth-aspergers-syndrome/.

On Oe, see Lindsley Cameron, *The Music of Light: The Extrarodinary Story of Hikari and Kenzaburo Oe* (New York: The Free Press, 1998). The quotation from the critic is on p. 125.

On cognition and atonal music, see for instance Diana Raffman, "Is Twelve-Tone Music Artistically Defective?" *Midwest Studies in Philosophy* (2003), 69–87, and the literature surveyed therein. One classic work is C. L. Krumhansl, *Cognitive Foundations of Musical Pitch* (New York: Oxford University Press, 1990) and also C. L. Krumhansl, G. J. Sandell, and D. C. Sergeant, "The Perception of Tone Hierarchies and Mirror Forms in Twelve-Tone Serial Music," *Music Perception* 5, no. 1 (1987), 31–78. See also Nicola Dibben, "The cognitive reality of hierarchic structure in tonal and atonal music," *Music Perception* 12 (1994), 1–25. I also am indebted to correspondence with Helen Daynes about her unpublished work in related areas and also to comments from Eric Lyon.

Arthur Danto's views on the Brillo box and related matters can be found in his *Beyond the Brillo Box: The Visual Arts in Post-Historical Perspective* (Berkeley: University of California Press, 1998).

The Asperger quotation is from Hans Asperger's essay "Autistic psychopathy in childhood," reprinted in Uta Frith, ed., *Autism and Asperger Syndrome* (Cambridge, UK: Cambridge University Press, 1991), 37–92; the particular quotation comes from pp. 72–73.

CHAPTER 9: AUTISTIC POLITICS

On the question of objectivity, see for instance Rita R. Jordan, "Practical implications of memory characteristics in autistic spectrum disorders," in *Memory and Autism,* edited by Jill Boucher and Dermot Bowler (Cambridge, UK: Cambridge University Press, 2008), 293–310; the quotation itself is from p. 305. On the economic experiment, see Benedetto De Martino, Neil A. Harrison, Steven Knafo, Geoff Bird, and Raymond J. Dolan, "Explaining Enhanced Logical Consistency During Decision Making in Autism," *Journal of Neuroscience* 28, no. 42 (October 15, 2008), 10746–50.

For Hayek's work in neurology, see *The Sensory Order: An Inquiry into the Foundations of Theoretical Psychology* (Chicago: University of Chicago Press, 1963 [1952]).

On Kant's teaching, see Roger J. Sullivan, *Immanuel Kant's Moral Theory* (Cambridge, UK: Cambridge University Press, 1989), 1; Manfred Kuehn, *Kant: A Biography* (Cambridge, UK: Cambridge University Press), 270–73, is one place to look for anecdotes about Kant.

On George Mikes and queuing, see Joe Moran, *Queuing for Beginners: The Story of Daily Life from Breakfast to Bedtime* (London: Profile Books, 2008), 61.

CHAPTER 10: THE FUTURE OF THE UNIVERSE

On information technology as used by autistics to communicate, one book is Dinah Murray and Ann Aspinall, *Getting IT: Using Information Technology to Empower People with Communication Difficulties* (Philadelphia: Jessica Kingsley Publishers, 2006).

See Olaf Stapledon, *Starmaker* (New York: St. Martin's Press, 1987 [1937]), 34–35.

On the Tony Attwood anecdote, see Benjamin Nugent, *American Nerd: The Story of My People* (New York: Scribner, 2008), 146.

For Grandin on Japan, see Temple Grandin, *The Way I See It: A Personal Look at Autism and Asperger's* (Arlington, TX: Future Horizons, 2008), 222.

On Finland, see Richard D. Lewis, *Finland, Cultural Lone Wolf* (Boston: Intercultural Press, 2007).

Jonathan Sacks is quoted in Deirdre N. McCloskey, *The Bourgeois Virtues: Ethics for an Age of Commerce* (Chicago: University of Chicago Press, 2007), 30.

The idea of manipulating stars to make them visible from a distance I have borrowed from Robin Hanson. On the Doritos ad, see freakonomics.blogs .nytimes.com/2008/03/19/et-the-entrepreneur.

My blog post on the Fermi Paradox can be found here: www.marginalrevolution .com/marginalrevolution/2008/05/the-fermi-parad.html.

ACKNOWLEDGMENTS

I have many debts, including, of course, to Kathleen Fasanella. I would like to offer particular thanks to Michelle Dawson for her comments on the manuscript and also for helping me to understand recent research on autism. Bryan Caplan offered useful comments on the manuscript, as did Autism Diva and Seth Roberts and my wife, Natasha. Parts of chapter 3 are drawn from much earlier conversations with Sahar Akhtar. Yana Chernyak offered help with some of the ideas in chapter 4. I thank Eric Lyon and Kiriana Cowansage for useful correspondence and ideas on music and aesthetics. The comments and feedback from my agent, Teresa Hartnett, and editor, Stephen Morrow, have been invaluable throughout. I have drawn on comments and conversations from many other people but I am not sure they all wish to be identified by name in this context, so I will offer them a very strong collective thanks.

INDEX